CW01653354

EVOLUTION OR HOW DID WE GET HERE?

The 11th 'Christ and the Cosmos' Publication

Others in the series:
"Christ and the Cosmos" (Conference year 1987)
"Christ and the Cosmos: Volume II" (1989)
"Chirst and the Cosmos: Volume III" (1990)
"Christ and the Cosmos: Mision and Complexity" (1991)
"Christ and the Cosmos: Interpreting the Cosmos" (1992)
"Christ and the Cosmos: Being Human in a Cosmic Context" (1993)
"Christ and the Cosmos: Being Responsible in aCosmic Context" (1994)
"Christ and the Cosmos: Members - One of Another" (1995)
"Christ and the Cosmos: The Image of the Invisible God (1996)
and
Taking the Initiative: Introductions and Extracts form the 'Christ and the Cosmos' Initiative writings (published 1993)

ISBN 0 9530360 1 4

EVOLUTION OR HOW DID WE GET HERE?

Volume XI in the "Christ and the Cosmos" Series

Proceedings of the Conference held at Westminster College, Oxford from 4th to 6th April 1997.

Edited by P.A. Beetham

1997 Conference Co-ordinator Professor A. Garner

Published by: The Christ and the Cosmos Initiative and Westminster College

Publication Team
Editor:
Rev. P.A. Beetham, B.A, B.Sc., Ph.D., C.Biol., M.I.Biol.

Sound Recording:
Mr. Rowland Budgen, M.Phil., B.Ed., F.I.M.L.S., M.I.Biol.

Copy Preparation:
Mrs. J. Beetham

Proof Reading:
Mr. J. Barratt, Ll.M.

Readers' comments and enquiries on this book or about the Initiative in general will be welcomed.

Please address any correspondence to The Editor at Trinity Manse, Tower Road, Felixstowe, Suffolk. IP11 7PR.

CONTENTS

Foreword

Darwinists are not necessarily hoofed and horned monsters, but are occasionally of pacific habits, and may even be detected in the act of going to church

Leslie Stephen, 'Darwinism and Divinity' in *Essays on Freethinking and Plainspeaking,* 1873

The controversy concerning Darwin's evolutionary theory has dominated the perceived argument between science and the Christian faith more than any other in the last century. Neo-Darwinism, that development of Darwin's theory which also embraces Mendel's theories of inheritance is the basis of modern systematic biology and the theory of evolution is accepted in most western societies as the explanation of human origin. It is a common perception that as evolutionary thinking has expanded the ground of theological Christian thinking has retreated, the two being seen in opposition. It is evident from the papers of this consultation that this apparent conflict is not inevitable. Much of the support for Darwin's ideas in the nineteenth century came from the church, whereas the atheist Soviet Union of Stalin's era was implacably opposed to them. It must be said however that the Church has not on the whole dealt well with Darwin's theory, failing to understand the nature of a scientific theory and often treating it as dogma. One important exception is found in Jürgen Moltmann's theology of creation presented in the Gifford Lectures of 1984-85.[1]

Legends abound concerning Darwin's own religious beliefs or lack of them.[2] A series of useful essays can be found in John Durrant's volume[3] which gives a broad ranging and scholarly account of the evidence.

In Darwin's lifetime, much to his own dismay his theory was applied to other areas of academic study, such as history, this process has continued so that today evolution is an important concept wherever development is considered. The lectures in this volume consider evolutionary ideas not only in biology and human evolution but also in culture, the origin of language and the development of religion.

---

[1] Moltmann, J., "God In Creation", The Gifford Lectures 1984-85, An ecological doctrine of creation, published SCM Press 1985. ISBN 0-334-00571-X.

[2] Moore, James, "The Darwin Legend - Are reports of his deathbed conversion true?", published Hodder & Stoughton 1995. ISBN 0-340-64243-2.

[3] Durant, J. (Editor), "Darwinism and Divinity", published Blackwell 1985. ISBN 0-631-14188-X.

CHARLES DARWIN
The ORIGIN of SPECIES

PART ONE
Lectures

Man's Place in Nature

Professor David M. Knight

Department of Philosophy, Durham University

The first theory of evolution to be successful in the scientific world was Charles Darwin's, published in his *Origin of Species* in 1859, and greatly promoted by Thomas Henry Huxley in the years which followed. Ultimately, Darwin was buried in Westminster Abbey; and Huxley was successively President of the British Association, and of the Royal Society: they had succeeded in their lifetimes in making their ideas acceptable, and their names had become household words. We still live in the world they inaugurated, and it is with them that an exploration of what is involved in an evolutionary world-view best begins.

Our title is that of a famous book by Huxley, published in 1863. Naturally there have been many new discoveries, for example of fossils; and Darwinian ideas have been much developed since then, notably through genetics: and it may seem perverse to go back over a hundred years if we want to consider evolution's importance for us. Three questions may be at the back of our minds: first, will such an approach be too historical?; second, will it be too academic?, and finally, how relevant will it be to us living in the late twentieth century and trying to make sense of faith and reason?

The evolution of evolution

Thinking about T.H. Huxley and his confrontations with Bishop Samuel Wilberforce, Professor Richard Owen, the Duke of Argyll, W.E. Gladstone and other worthies of the Victorian age may seem antiquarian; but over a century later, we live in an age where 'Creationist' opposition to Darwinism is very prominent - notably in the USA, and in Australia. Clearly if there is a war here - and Huxley's rhetoric was certainly belligerent - it has been a hundred years war, and we have little hope of understanding the latest skirmishes unless we go back to the beginning. When we do, we shall find that whereas there was much technical opposition to Darwin in what Huxley called ‘the Church Scientific’, most of which now seems dated and fully answered; the important issues in connection with science and religion were identified at the outset, and remain with us.

Huxley’s particular importance was as a spokesman, ‘an incomparable literary swordsman’ as one disciple described him. From the lower middle class, making his way through a medical training at Charing Cross Hospital on scholarships, attending to the needy, and contemptuous of the establishment; he joined the Royal Navy as an assistant surgeon. His talent was spotted, and he was sent on a survey voyage on board *HMS Rattlesnake*, in Australian waters, under Captain Owen Stanley. His reputation as a scientist was made with his studies of marine invertebrates netted on the voyage; and in Sydney he met his future wife.

Back in England, needing time to write up his discoveries, he left the Navy and lived precariously for some years; precociously elected a Fellow of the Royal Society, he found it very difficult to get a full-time job in science. Owen became his patron, and then, in trying to patronise him, his antagonist: Huxley certainly had a chip on his shoulder, but particularly resented the powerful position the clergy still retained in the 1850s and ‘60s in the educational world. With his friends John Tyndall the physicist, Edward Frankland the chemist, Joseph Hooker the future Director of Kew, and others he formed the X-club; which worked as a pressure-group promoting the interests of meritocrats and agnostics (Huxley’s word) in the Church Scientific. Eventually all these found posts in London, and achieved great eminence as science became something like a profession in Victorian Britain, rather than an avocation for gentlemen.

The Census of 1851 showed that only half the population of Britain were churchgoers: churches and chapels had in effect lost the urban working class. For Huxley organised religion was part of a system which kept people like him down, and his country backward; and Darwinian theory gave him a splendid stick with which to beat it. He hoped to inaugurate what he sometimes called a New Reformation, in which clergy would be duly put in their place - the new presbyter joining the old priest in limbo, as ordinary lay people took responsibility for their lives. An open mind about undecidable questions, like all those to do with God, was essential; agnosticism and science for him went together. 'Trained and organised common sense' (the adjectives are important) rather than dogma was the key to knowledge. The cholera might indeed be recognised as a plague sent from God - but as a punishment for ignorance, dirt, and neglect of science, rather than for breaking the Ten Commandments.

In the USA, in the wake of Reconstruction after the Civil War, Darwinism was imposed upon the defeated rednecks of the Bible Belt by carpet-bagging Yankees; and a fundamentalist 'Creationism' has become the populist option. In Britain, Huxley the plebeian made evolution the populist doctrine; while his effete opponents from the establishment clung to a more liberal form of the doctrine that the Earth and its inhabitants were created by God. Huxley was never very sympathetic to natural selection: like all the best disciples he had an independent attitude to his master's teaching. But like his friend Tyndall, in his celebrated Belfast Address to the British Association for the Advancement of Science in 1874, he saw evolutionary theory as meaning that there was no longer any need for the hypothesis of a Creator. Atomic theory and evolution between them promised to leave no gaps for God.

Philip Gosse, in his notorious *Omphalos* of 1858, had argued that just as Adam and Eve would have had navels though they had not had mothers, so the Earth might contain fossils although it had never had dinosaurs; they were signs of an apparent, not a real, history. But because they were sophisticated graduates, Huxley's opponents did not mostly believe in the literal truth of *Genesis 1 or 2*. They interpreted 'In the beginning' to cover the first millions of years before mankind appeared on the scene; or the days of creation to be each a thousand ages: Huxley had some fun with such elastic hermeneutics. Nevertheless, as the dust settled and by the time Darwin died in 1882, there were many who were content with a theistic interpretation of evolution; seeing God as working his purpose out in a long process of development, rather than designing each and every kind of barnacle to fit its niche. By this time also, evolutionary ideas had taken such hold that in fields remote from biology they were being applied: in the wake perhaps of J.H. Newman's pre-Darwinian essay on the development of doctrine.

When the snobbish Wilberforce asked Huxley if it was on his grandfather's or grandmother's side that he claimed descent from an ape, Huxley is supposed to have told his neighbour 'The Lord hath delivered him into mine hand' - he loved Biblical rhetoric. His riposte, and the exact form of words used is in considerable doubt, was that of a good plebeian: what matters in judging people is how they live, not who their ancestors were. Huxley was well aware of the importance of being earnest; and thus turned the tables on his opponent, who was seen to have made a frivolous contribution to a serious debate, unlike a true gentleman.

Not long afterwards, Pooh-Bah was to bask in the glory of his descent from protoplasm: but in real life, Huxley, armed with evolutionary theory, assailed not only the Bishop but also the Goliath of deference.

Where Wilberforce was closer to modern sensibilities was in his attitude to racism: it was a part of his family tradition (as it was of Darwin's) which he fully shared, that we are all brothers under the skin, and that no humans are more half-akin to ape than others. By the standards of his day Huxley was not a racist, but he shared the assumptions of most Victorian Englishmen; and since 'Social Darwinism' cannot be disentangled from other kinds, evolutionary theory could encourage those who looked in alarm at 'degenerates' in their own society, and with indifference at tribesmen dying out when faced with the manifest destiny of their civilised competitors. Here as elsewhere, the story is ongoing.

What I hope all this indicates is that we live in the shadow of the past, bearing the load it has imposed upon us; and if we therefore infer that the ultimate explanation in human affairs is historical, it is necessary thus to go back and gain an historical perspective. We still have bossy clergy, and aggressive scientists like Richard Dawkins whose career has been much advanced by his playing the part of Huxley; we have Creationists not unlike Gosse; we have snobs and meritocrats, and racists. History can cast light upon them all.

A Recondite And Technical Matter?

Much science is a closed book to the layman. Scientific training has a dogmatic character; children are taught to describe their experiments in the flat but authoritative language of the passive voice and the abstract noun; jargon and algebra deter trespassers in this territory. But it need not be so; and here again Huxley and Darwin were their own popularisers, and can make for us the points we need to think about.

In his accessible book, *Man's Place in Nature*, Huxley imagined a scientific visitor from Saturn (the Seventh Heaven?) who had come to Earth to study our fauna. In grouping similar species (like sheep and goats; or horses, donkeys and zebras) into classes, he would put humans, gorillas, chimpanzees and orang-utans together, because of their many resemblances and relatively small differences. We should in Huxley's view aim for similar detachment: looking at our fellow-men, from the scientific point of view, much as we would contemplate marine invertebrates.

That book was prompted by his encounter with Owen at the 1860 BAAS meeting in Oxford, a few days before the debate with Wilberforce. Huxley always loved a fight; and when addressing establishment audiences, as at the Royal Institution, he enjoyed teasing them, biting the hand that fed him, showing his sharpened beak and claws. Rather differently, he took his students (in institutions which were ancestors of Imperial College) through a very factual study of the crayfish, in which its evolution only occupied the last 10% of the course, and was presented as hypothetical. He was at his most genial and relaxed in lectures to working men, where there was no syllabus to be got through and where he could draw them in like a lawyer making a case to a jury. He never spoke down, or patronised these audiences. One of the most celebrated lectures is on a piece of chalk: this least sophisticated of teaching aids (he was famous for his sketching on the blackboard) provided him with a starting point to run through the fossil record. Having supplied facts, he invited his audience to come to their own conclusion: "Choose your hypothesis; I have chosen mine. I can find no warranty for believing in the distinct creation of a score of successive species of crocodiles in the course of countless ages of time. Science gives no countenance to such a wild fancy; nor can the perverse ingenuity of a commentator pretend to discover this sense, in the simple words with which the writer of Genesis records the proceedings of the fifth end sixth days of the Creation."

The sequence of species, brought to the attention of his unschooled audience, could be explained in no other way than by evolution; unless one deserted the scientific goal of using natural analogies in explanation.

He ended with a splendid peroration, bringing in the powerful metaphor of illumination: "A small beginning has led us to a great ending. If I were to put the bit of chalk with which we started into the hot but obscure flame of burning hydrogen, it would presently shine like the sun. It seems to me that this physical metamorphosis is no false image for what has been the result of our subjecting it to a jet of fervent, though nowise brilliant, thought tonight. It has become luminous, and its clear rays, penetrating the abyss of the remote past, have brought within our ken some stages of the evolution of the earth."

Young Huxley had turned his pinafore round and preached to his sisters; for him, professing was a performance art, and he could communicate not only enthusiasm but also the essence of scientific discovery and theory.

Darwin was not like Huxley a preacher manqué, but he had set out on his voyage, on *HMS Beagle*, as an ordinand taking a year or two out to see the world before finding a pleasant country parish where he could be a latter-day Gilbert White. The collections and letters he sent back during the voyage meant that he returned to find himself a celebrated man of science; and reading Thomas Malthus' *Essay on Population* (1798) gave him the key to evolution by natural selection. Engaging with William Paley's *Natural Theology* (1802) he used a similar structure of argument. In a sermon of apologetic, or a manifesto, there is no chain of deductive reasoning (as in Euclid's geometry) where each proposition leads inexorably to the next; and where a single weak link will cause the chain to break. Nor is there careful inductive generalisation from some well-authenticated instances. Instead we find a rope, twisted from various arguments of varying strength and plausibility, which together will support a weight far greater than any could bear on their own; and if one such fibre should snap, the rope will probably still hold.

While collecting evidence for development over many years, Darwin took time out to write the standard work on barnacles, living and fossil. In part, this may have been a displacement activity. He had an explosive idea, and could estimate the row it would cause were he to publish, from the furious reviews, and enormous publicity, attracted by the anonymous evolutionary book, *Vestiges of the Natural History of Creation* (1844). Another reason might be that hitherto he was known as 'Mr Darwin the traveller'; a speculative book by such a person would not be treated with the same respect as one written by the greatest living authority on some group of obscure creatures. The right to speculate in science is earned by solid previous research.

But over and above these things is the consideration that the barnacles were an interesting group, which under Darwin's hand and eye proved even more interesting. It was not long before he set out on *HMS Beagle* that J.V. Thompson, a naval surgeon stationed in Ireland, had proved that barnacles are related to shrimps, crabs and lobsters. Their young are free-swimming, and look like little shrimps; only in middle age do they settle down and fix themselves to a rock, jetty or ship. They thus adopt a life-style like that of limpets, a much simpler kind of creature.

For Darwin, development was open-ended. Under the pressure of natural selection, competing with their siblings, animals and plants diverged to fill suitable niches. For Lamarck and most previous evolutionists, the process had a direction: it was moving upwards, towards ever-greater complexity, and culminating in us (anyway, so far). Darwin avoided the word 'evolution' in the early editions of the *Origin* (though the last word is 'evolved') because of these directional implications. Like anyone in Victorian society, a creature could go down as well as up in the world; and barnacles had moved down, to live like limpets instead of like crabs. This had been immensely successful; there are enormous numbers of barnacles of many different kinds. They came to dominate the Darwin household, so that when the children went out to tea they are supposed to have asked 'Where does your father do his barnacles?'

One of Darwin's most exciting discoveries was that in some species of barnacle, the male has further degenerated so that he is just a stomach and sex-organs, living within the shell of the female - a way of life remote from Victorian values. Here was a stunning confirmation of his intuition that there was no direction to evolution. He became reluctant to speak of 'higher' and 'lower' organisms, as had come naturally to thinkers since Aristotle, who had placed organisms on a scale, chain or ladder with humans at the top (perhaps surmounted by angels in their various array). For Darwin, species are successful insofar as they are adjusted to their environment at a particular time. If that environment is unchanging, as we know of the coelacanth's at the bottom of the Indian Ocean, then no evolution will happen. The lack of a clear direction to the process of development, with its apparently chancy reliance upon natural selection, was a major problem for strict Darwinians; and while most people were evolutionists in late Victorian Britain, most thought it had a direction: they were allies rather than disciples of Darwin. Henry Drummond's book, *The Ascent of Man* (1894) encapsulates this way of thinking.

Darwin's study of barnacles does not make easy reading, but his work on pigeon-fancying, his books on orchids and on earthworms, and his *Descent of Man* (1871) as well as the *Origin* did strike a more popular chord. Pigeons had been diversified into breeds so different that if they had been found wild they would have been put into separate genera, not just species. The curious forms of orchids could be accounted for if they had evolved in step with the insect which fertilises them; and the lowly worm plays an essential ecological role. In the *Descent,* Darwin introduced the idea of sexual selection to account for the peacock's tail: peahens will mate only with the most beautiful male, and since leaving descendants (rather than surviving) is what evolution is about, extravagant tails will naturally have been selected. Characteristics of only one sex, that are not directly concerned with reproduction (like men's beards) can be thus accounted for.

In the *Origin*, there is a famous passage where Darwin connects clover and cats: clover is fertilised by bumble bees; they are preyed upon by field mice; which in turn are controlled by cats, which in turn are kept by people. So we can see that in the writings of the pioneers of evolution, the implications of the idea were worked out and made clear even to those who would have little understanding of the technical treatises which both Darwin and Huxley also wrote. They had the gift of making science compelling; of picking upon the really interesting features of their subject of study.

Relevance To Life.

For Huxley, evolution was promoted as part of an anti-Christian campaign to rid the world of superstition and ignorance; for Darwin it was not. But well before the *Origin* was published, the problem of pain was vividly presented by Tennyson in his great poem, *In Memoriam*:

"Man,
Who trusted God was love indeed
And love Creation's final law -
Tho' Nature, red in tooth and claw
With ravine, shriek'd against his creed."

Pain may for humans be redemptive, though often suffering does not ennoble us; but it is hard to contemplate with equanimity all the pain and grief which has gone into the evolutionary process, notably among animals: - 'the Dragons of the prime, that tare each other in their slime'. For Paley, the wolf was a euthanasia machine: it quickly polished off the ageing gazelle which would otherwise have become arthritic, and the sum of happiness in the world was thus increased by carnivores. For Darwin, the competition is no longer between wolves and their prey, but between wolves: more are born than can survive, and the battle goes to the stronger.

Darwin's theory was closely tied to what was happening in Britain, the first industrial nation, in his lifetime: and nature for him resembles what we call the Real World. In the Bible, this is the World: but we call it real nowadays, in case anyone should subscribe to the Buddhist intuition that it is an illusion, rather than something worshipful - real, réal, royal. In the Real World, there is little love lost; we are all in competition, the weakest go to the wall, and early birds rather than lame ducks get the worm. An ethic based upon naturalism would encourage the strong at the expense of the weak, as in social Darwinism: the most able bodied get into the boat, and then it is 'Cast off Jack, I'm all right' as the *Titanic* sinks, freighted with the young, the infirm, and the self-sacrificing.

In his last years, Huxley in a famous series of Romanes Lectures distanced himself from these ethical consequences of scientific naturalism. He had always loved the language and imagery of the Bible, and he came greatly to admire the Old Testament prophets for their courage and their insight into the human condition. Elijah denouncing the wicked Jezebel and Ahab; Jeremiah flung into a well but sticking to his unpopular message of judgement; these were rôle models for the plebeian sage and moralist who believed his country was in mortal danger through its neglect of science. Society, for the older Huxley as for the young medical student, was to be judged by the way it treated the weak and defenceless; having understood the process of evolution, we shall progress by defying rather than submitting to the survival of the fittest in the struggle for existence.

The scientists (the word was coined in 1832, by analogy with *artist*) of the nineteenth century were the offspring not only of the Enlightenment, but also of the Romantic Movement. Nature for them was not just Paley's watch, an 'it' whose workings were to be mastered, but a 'she' to be wooed and worshipped in appreciation of the beautiful and the sublime. In an effusion of uncertain date, Humphry Davy (chemist, inventor of the safety lamp, President of the Royal Society) wrote:

"Oh, most magnificent and noble nature!

Have I not worshipped thee with such a love

As never mortal man before displayed?

Adored thee in thy majesty of visible creation,

And searched into thy hidden and mysterious ways

As Poet, as Philosopher, as Sage?"

He had also written of the chemist in his laboratory exerting a god-like creative power: Victor (later victim) Frankenstein's teacher was modelled upon Davy. Under S.T. Coleridge's tutelage, the young Davy had had 'an experience of nature', when everything seemed alive and it would have given him pain to pick a leaf from a tree. Davy loved the Julian Alps; and similarly Tyndall was a zealous mountaineer (his ice-axe is preserved in the museum in Zermatt) who delighted in the sublime experience of nature among the summits.

James Glaisher the meteorologist 'experienced the sense of sublimity and awe' on a balloon flight (soon after the *Origin* was published), and believed it was 'the intellectual yearning after the knowledge of the Creator, and an involuntary faith acknowledging the immortality of the soul'. In going from nature to nature's God, he was more closely following the steps of William Paley, whose writings on natural theology were the only part of the formal Cambridge syllabus that were of any use to the young Darwin: even if his conclusions were somewhat less orthodox. Nature working through natural selection, trial and error, was less worshipful than the many-breasted and nurturing goddess of Antiquity. Indeed it seemed as though David Hume might have been right, that she 'poured forth from her womb, without discernment or maternal care, her maimed and abortive children'. King Alfonso of Castile, faced with the epicycles of Ptolemaic astronomy, is supposed to have remarked that if God had him consulted about the creation, he would have recommended something different: for different reasons, those faced with Darwin's real world might have said the same. Darwin thought that it was more worthy of God to have started a process leading to the present state of things, than to have made a world which required constant interference or renewal; but not everybody would agree. But at least Darwin's was not an inanimate cold world, like that of the Enlightenment.

Seeing ourselves as the outcome of a blind and directionless process is humbling; and seeing purposes or ends in nature has become more difficult since 1859. But a reflective Huxley later wrote that Darwin had brought teleology back into biology. To him and his colleagues in the 1840s and '50s, it had been impossible to use the language of purpose which had come so readily to naturalists ever since Aristotle. Paley had remarked on how well designed and happy animals were in their various habitats; but giving God a pat on the back for a well-thought-out tooth or claw was no longer appropriate. Armed with the *Origin*, the scientist could once again ask what was the use or value of an organ; rephrasing this if pressed in terms of survival value in a harshly competitive world. Darwin's family laughed at him for writing advertisements for the creatures he was enthusiastically describing; barnacles, orchids or earthworms.

Darwinian evolution thus introduced us to an open-ended cosmos, in which it could no longer be said that

"Yea, the first Morning of Creation wrote
What the Last Dawn of Reckoning shall read."

The laws of chance, codified in the nineteenth century into statistical explanation, were shown by James Clerk Maxwell (also in 1859) to cover the behaviour of molecules in gases, unless a demon were to interfere with them; and they govern Darwin's world. We cannot predict what will happen in future evolution. We use purposive language and understanding of ourselves and other people; with less certainty, we can use it of animals; and as a metaphor, even of plants spreading their leaves. But it is no longer easy to see any purposes beyond our own; or to see a moral universe outside our societies. A scientific clerisy has arisen in Huxley's and Tyndall's wake: the gaps available for God to fill have shrunk; but the improbability of our evolving, and the implausibility of sociobiology in explaining our subjective existences, make naturalism an enormous leap of faith.

Huxley thus put a finger on the morality and the purposiveness of evolution; and at the time of his death in 1895 was wrestling with the writings of A.J. Balfour, who had taken up Newton's question, 'Whence comes all the order and beauty we see in the world?'. It did not seem to Balfour enough to tell stories about arousing the lust of peahens to explain our delight in the beauty of nature, and of art. Nor did he believe that evolution would guarantee what we demand, true beliefs about the world: survival value might in a general way be tied to truth, but not necessarily so. Darwin's ally A.R. Wallace could see that being able to count - knowing that there was still one wolf left inside the cave - would have survival value; but found our capacity for pure mathematics inexplicable in evolutionary terms. What they valued most highly - morality, truth, beauty and abstract thinking - seemed to those pondering them at the end of the nineteenth century to be irreducible to evolutionary explanations. We now have sociobiology and evolutionary psychology; but whether these are any closer to providing a complete evolutionary account of humanity seems very doubtful.

Further Reading.

P. Bowler, *Charles Darwin: the man and his influence, Cambridge U.P., 2nd ed., Cambridge U.P., 1996.*

J.H. Brooke, *Science and Religion: some historical perspectives, Cambridge U.P., 1991.*

J. Browne, *Charles Darwin: Voyaging, Jonathan Cape, 1995.*

R. Dawkins, *The Blind Watchmaker, Penguin, 1991.*

A. Desmond, *Huxley: the Devil's Disciple, Michael Joseph, 1994.*

A. Desmond & J.R. Moore, *Darwin, Michael Joseph, 1992.*

D.M. Knight, `Getting Science Across', *British Journal for the History of Science, 29 (1996), 129-38.*

D.M. Knight, *Humphry Davy: Science and Power, 2nd ed., Cambridge UP., 1997.*

M. Shortland & R. Yeo, *Telling Lives in Science: essays on scientific biography, Cambridge U.P., 1996.*

K. Ward, *God, Chance & Necessity, One World, 1996.*

RECENT DISCOVERIES AND DEVELOPMENTS IN HUMAN EVOLUTION

Professor Alan Bilsborough

Department of Anthropology, University of Durham

Introduction

The discovery of human antiquity practically coincided with Darwin's exposition of evolution by natural selection. The *annus mirabilis* of 1859 saw the publication of the *Origin of Species*, the discovery of cave men in the Perigord and the confirmation of claims for early man contemporary with extinct animals in the Somme terraces. Just three years earlier the first recognised human fossil -from Neanderthal - had been recovered, building upon the find from Gibraltar in 1848.

Over the next century increasing evidence was discovered in Europe, S.E. and Continental Asia, and Southern Africa. It was not until 1959 that the first significant early hominid find was made in East Africa, but since that time the rate of recovery has snowballed. Fossil evidence recovered in the last two decades greatly exceeds all that found before, so that we now have a much more complete view of human evolution than only 20 or 25 years ago. In this paper I want to summarise some major aspects of the evolutionary record, with a particular emphasis on recent discoveries and the ways in which they have changed perceptions of the patterns and processes of human evolution.

It is not just a question of filling in details via the fossil record - quite the reverse: the expanded evidence points to a radically different picture from earlier interpretations. Most fundamentally, the pattern of human evolution is now viewed as a radiating bush with many branches, rather than a tree with a few major limbs and a single main trunk leading to modern humans. Many more hominid species are now widely recognised (at 18 a trebling compared with just two decades ago) and since there can only have been one particular evolutionary pathway to modern humans, tracing its route within this complex array becomes increasingly difficult as species multiply. Another corollary of this model is that most earlier species became extinct: extinction has been the norm for hominid, as well as non-hominid, species. A further, perhaps not so obvious, implication is that there was nothing inevitable in the evolution and appearance of our species: in Stephen Gould's telling phrase '*Homo sapiens* is an entity, not a tendency.'

Hominid Origins and Early Evolution

Modern humans and their immediate fossil relatives are included within the Primate family Hominidae consisting of two main genera - *Australopithecus* and *Homo* - to which a third genus, *Ardipithecus*, has recently been added (see below). The origin, characteristics and evolutionary relationships of the earliest hominids are poorly known. There was an extensive radiation of primitive apes in the widespread forest and woodland of the Early and Middle Miocene (20-12 million years ago (mya)), but then cooler, drier, more seasonal conditions resulted in dwindling tree cover, expanding grassland and the extinction of all but a handful of ape species. The stem lineage of African apes and hominids presumably evolved during this period (12 -8 mya), but there is virtually no fossil evidence to document this immediate pre-hominid phase.

Most workers agree that hominids split from the African ape lineage(s) in the period 6-8 mya, although relevant sites and fossil evidence are lacking. The pressures underlying the split are similarly unknown, although a dietary shift, perhaps to more ground or shrub vegetation following increased competition for the declining fruits and other tree products within the contracting forest, was probably involved. Early hominids tend to have smaller anterior teeth (incisors and canines) and larger cheek teeth (premolars and molars) with thicker enamel than their ape relatives. They also display a distinctive combination of vertical and lateral jaw movements, producing rotary chewing, rather than the mainly vertical chomping of apes. All this points to increased crushing and grinding in early hominids compared with apes.

At around their time of origin or somewhat later hominids evolved a distinctive ground dwelling adaptation - bipedal locomotion. For a long period this appears to have been combined with tree living, and was perhaps used mainly for standing during feeding and for moving only short distances from tree to tree, or when crossing glades and clearings. It is perhaps better to speak of bipedalism*s*, for there were doubtless several early locomotor modes, all different from the long distance, striding bipedalism that typifies modern humans.

The earliest hominid fossil (a mandible from Lothagam Hill, Kenya) is about 5.6 mya, and there is another, rather younger, mandible at 5 mya from Tabarin, Kenya. In general, finds are very few and far between until around 4 mya. Dating from 4.4 mya , and so just before that watershed, is the recently discovered and remarkably primitive *Ardipithecus ramidus* from Ethiopia. This is very chimp-like in its dentition, and probably represents a relict form, approximating to hominids in the 6-7 mya range rather than typifying the general run of hominid morphology at just over 4 mya. Its forelimb was long and powerfully muscled, and there is fossil evidence of the trunk and hind limb, although these are not yet described.

Between 3 and 4 mya there is evidence of progressive, more obviously hominid species - *Australopithecus anamensis* (4 mya) and the rather younger *A. afarensis,* including the famous 'Lucy' specimen (3.2-3.7 mya), both from East Africa, and *A. africanus* (2.4 - 3+ mya) in South Africa. There is also the recently discovered *A. bahrelghazali* from Chad, some 2500 km west of the Rift Valley and so all the other hominid fossils, indicating that early hominids were much more widely distributed then previously thought. Where known, all these forms show adaptations to bipedal locomotion in their pelvis and hindlimbs, and there is definite behavioural evidence for bipedalism in the form of the famous Laetoli footprints. However, it was not of the modern striding kind, and upper trunk and arm remains still show climbing adaptations. In fact, all these early hominid species are found in contexts that indicate significant tree cover and woodland, at least in the immediate vicinity. Early hominids were thus tied to treed habitats, and although widely distributed, probably represent an array of multiple, closely related species rather than just one or two widely distributed forms, for every break in tree cover would impede gene flow and so promote speciation.

Within this broad array is a distinctive later group (1.2-2.5 mya) of forms with massive face and jaws, reinforced skulls, and greatly expanded cheek teeth with further emphasis on crushing and grinding - the robust australopithecines. One, and possibly two species (*A. robustus* and *A. crassidens*) are known from South Africa, and two from East Africa (*A. aethiopicus* and A. *boisei*). While displaying the same general features, they differ in anatomical details, suggesting they were independent (parallel) developments in response to common habitat pressures rather than a single lineage. Climatic change was probably a major factor in their origin and radiation. A distinct glacial phase around 2.4-2.5 mya resulted in drier, more seasonal conditions across much of Africa, reducing tree cover yet further and promoting the shift to extended ground dwelling. Some workers prefer to incorporate the robusts in a separate genus *Paranthropus* to reflect their common features and discrete radiation.

Early *Homo*

From before 2 mya the fossil record indicates another distinct radiation, overlapping with that of the robusts spatially and temporally. This radiation consists of forms with smaller faces and jaws, more equal dental proportions and (generally) more lightly constructed brain cases with some cranial expansion - the characteristics of early *Homo.* By 2 mya three early *Homo* species are known from East and South Africa: *H. habilis, H.rudolfensis* and the earliest examples of *H.erectus*. *H. habilis* has rather progressive face, jaws and teeth, and shows some brain expansion. However, below the neck it appears to have been remarkably primitive, resembling the much earlier 'Lucy' and displaying clear arboreal adaptations. Its habitat was evidently still a treed one. *H.rudolfensis* was rather bigger brained, but with a broad, flat strongly built face and jaws, and comparatively large teeth. Postcranial evidence is lacking, and so its locomotion is unknown.

H. erectus combines modest face, jaws and dentition with further brain expansion within a remarkably strongly constructed brain case. Thanks above all to the Turkana boy skeleton - the most complete early hominid fossil ever recovered - we know it to have been ruggedly built and strongly muscled, but essentially modern overall, with trunk and legs consistent with striding bipedalism as in modern humans, and no arboreal features of torso, shoulders or forelimbs. In terms of body proportions these *erectus* individuals were tall and linear, like modern humans such as the Nuer & Dinka in hot, dry habitats, reinforcing the evidence from anatomy that, unlike earlier hominids and *habilis*, they display committed adaptations to a terrestrial niche in hot, open savannah environments.

What does it mean to call all these forms *Homo* rather than *Australopithecus*? Probably not very much. The lower limit of the genus *Homo* is a rough and imprecise boundary (or rather several boundaries), fixed at various times by different workers on the basis of arbitrary thresholds of brain size, of face, jaw and tooth proportions, and in some instances on assumptions about tool-making and 'advanced' behaviour. The contrasting features of the three species suggest that they are not especially closely related, and may well have crossed this arbitrary *Homo* threshold independently. Two of the three species show undoubted australopithecine features - *rudolfensis* in face and jaws, *habilis* below the neck. In fact, *habilis* may well eventually turn out to be a cranially rather progressive, but late and essentially relict, australopithecine.

Only early *erectus* looks to deserve fully inclusion within *Homo*. The evolution of its distinctively modern, terrestrially adapted morphology by 2 mya suggests an origin well before that date. In fact, the discovery of an early *Homo* palate from Hadar, Ethiopia dated to 2.33 mya has recently been announced. This specimen, unnervingly catalogued as 666-1, provides the earliest evidence known of human palatal and dental proportions.

Tools, Behaviour and Cognition

The AL 666 palate is also associated with stone tools, and these are known from several other sites in East Africa from about 2.5 mya. Only a very few pre-date 2 mya, but after that time the record progressively expands. In most cases the evidence is localised and sparse, but at Olduvai in Tanzania sites are denser and the record richer. Despite the usual name Oldowan or 'pebble tool industries', the overwhelming bulk of these assemblages consists of thin concentrations of sharp flakes, and the pebble tools appear to have been simply the means for achieving the flakes. Some chimp groups are now known to make and use stone tools, and despite being labelled by archaeologists into categories such as scrapers, spheroids, picks etc., the general view now is that these apparently discrete Oldowan tool forms are simply successive stages in the reduction of cores as more and more flakes are removed. There is no imposition of form, and so no evidence of any mental template in their production. Nonetheless, the archaeological record does indicate behaviour more advanced than that shown by tool-making chimps, although this is not in the form of the artefacts, but in their transportation. At Olduvai some tools are made on material for which the nearest known sources are >10 km away, and around Koobi Fora, reconstructing cores from flakes - akin to doing three-dimensional jig-saws - shows the former to be incomplete. In other words, the cores were being brought to the site pre-struck, and in at least some cases taken away to be used again elsewhere. This conservation and transportation of raw material - generally referred to as 'curation'- is quite unknown with chimps, where tools are always made at the place of use from materials immediately available. The early hominid pattern implies significant transport, knowledge of resources in the general locality, not just immediate vicinity, and has been memorably described as indicating 'an ape level of intelligence, but an ape level pushed to its very limits.'

After about 1.5 mya the archaeological record becomes richer, with more and larger sites. Flakes -sharp or retouched - remain by far the most numerous items, and there are cobbles and hammer stones, but we also begin to get pear or tear shaped Acheulean handaxes. These are more regularly fashioned and with their symmetry (both left to right and front to back) are generally regarded as representing significant cognitive advance. Around this time *H. habilis* and *H. rudolfensis* disappear from the fossil record, and slightly later the robust australopithecines vanish, leaving *H. erectus* as the sole hominid form. Over the next million years or so the African record is one of progressive expansion into more varied habitats with larger occupation sites, more evidence of internal differentiation of activities, and greater ranges travelled. For example, before 1 mya we have evidence of human occupation of the Ethiopian highlands, with artefacts transported >100 km from their sources of origin.

Expansion beyond Africa

As well as progressive expansion into varied habitats within Africa, this period also sees hominid expansion beyond that continent, with early finds from the Middle East (Israel), Georgia, continental Asia (China) and Indonesia (Java). In fact, the timing of hominid entry into Asia is currently contested: there have been claims for very early fossil hominids (c1.8 mya or before) from Georgia, China and Java. While all such early claims can be criticised on various grounds (mainly dating uncertainties), if subsequently verified they will force us to recast all our ideas about human origins in Africa as well as the date(s) of expansion beyond.

In any event, there is good evidence of *Homo* in west Asia (Israel) by around 1.4 mya and in China and Java by at least 1.1-1.2 mya. Whatever the timing, the expansion of hominids into higher latitudes, where the climatic fluctuations of the Pleistocene would have been more pronounced, must have presented hominids with new adaptive challenges. For most of this period higher latitudes were presumably only occupied during warm interglacial phases, with groups retreating towards the tropics during glacial conditions.

Europe seems to have been occupied comparatively late. The earliest fossils are the recently discovered specimens from Gran Dolina (TD 6), Atapuerca, north Spain, dating to >0.8 mya, but too fragmentary to identify closely. They possibly represent *H. erectus,* or something very like it: they have recently been used as the basis for a new species - *H. antecessor* - or they may be early examples of the rather better known European form *H. heidelbergensis.* Specimens assigned to this species are mainly less than 0.5 mya, with a particularly large and highly variable sample from another Atapuerca site - the Sima des Huesos (Pit of Bones). These and the other European fossils are interesting because they show the presence of distinctive regional features not found elsewhere - double arched brow ridge, projecting mid-face with inflated cheek region, long mandible body, 'bun' on rear of skull - and others that are individually present from the TD 6 specimens onwards, but which regularly appear in combination from about 125,000 years onwards as part of the distinctive Neanderthal pattern. In other words many Neanderthal features appear to have evolved slowly over much of the Middle Pleistocene, before coalescing as part of a bigger brained, longer vaulted more lightly constructed skull morphology that we think of as Neanderthal.

Postcranially Neanderthals were short, stocky, barrel-chested, well muscled and very powerful individuals, with body proportions that, by cutting down on their surface area to mass ratio, would be adaptive for conserving heat in cold environments - the reverse of the tropically adapted African *erectus.* This climatic adaptation appears to be the case even in the Middle East, where characteristic Neanderthal morphology and proportions are known from sites between c. 100,000 and 40,000 years ago. This southern tongue of Neanderthal distribution links via the Caucasus and Crimea with their main geographical range (Europe and the southern CIS), and presumably represents Neanderthal groups pushed southwards by the expanding ice-sheets of the last glaciation.

However, it is not possible to account for all aspects of Neanderthal anatomy in functional and adaptive terms, and their features may in part represent the outcome of some reduced population bottleneck - perhaps in the cold phase around 150-180,000 years ago. This narrowed and distorted morphological range compared with preceding populations such as those indicated by the earlier European material, so producing the Neanderthals who thus represent physically powerful, cold-adapted archaic human groups with their own particular features due to bottlenecking.

What of modern human origins? The earliest evidence of individuals broadly like ourselves comes from sub-Saharan Africa and the Middle East. At the extreme southern tip of Africa the site of Klasies River has provided fragmentary remains of modern humans dated between 90-120,000 years, while Border Cave in Natal and sites in the Omo of southern Ethiopia and in the Sudan have also yielded modern fossils estimated to be around 90,000 years and > 70,000 years. Analysis of genetic diversity in modern populations on balance also points to an African origin, but using the genetic data to retrace evolutionary patterns requires certain far-reaching assumptions e.g. that selection is not acting on the genetic markers, and that mutation rates can be measured precisely. Given these constraints, the genetic evidence can, at best, only be supplemental. In any case, there is no reason to suppose that the origin and subsequent geographical spread of the particular short DNA sequences analysed in these genetic studies necessarily coincides with the spread of *morphologically* modern humans - the genetic data could reflect expansion beyond Africa at any time(s) from the earliest *H. erectus* onwards.

In the Middle East the Skhul rock shelter on Mt. Carmel and the nearby site of Jebel Qafzeh contained muscular, big-faced but otherwise broadly modern skeletal remains dated respectively to 80-100,000 years and 95,000 years. Neanderthals are known in the region down to c 40,000 years ago, indicating extensive chronological overlap. Similar, but less extensive overlap is known in Europe, where the earliest modern fossils are 35-40,000 years (central & eastern Europe) and about 5 - 10,000 years younger in the west. Here Neanderthal fossils are known down to c 34,000 (St Cesaire, sw France) and even 25,000-30,000 years in southern Spain (Zaffaryah and Gibraltar). This overlap of two distinctive morphologies with no convincing evidence of intermediates is strong evidence that, whatever the actual degree or otherwise of genetic exclusiveness, Neanderthals and moderns were acting as separate species, with minimal breeding contact. Additional, direct, evidence for this has recently been strikingly provided by the recovery of distinctive mitochondrial DNA (i.e. well outside the range of modern human variability) from the Neanderthal skeleton itself.

Moderns are also known by fossil evidence from SE Australia by 30,000 years ago, and from archaeological evidence in the north of the continent possibly 20,000 years earlier. Their presence there, and at the opposite periphery of the Old World in western Europe at about the same time points to much earlier origin in more central regions. As noted above, current fossil evidence suggests Africa for the early appearance of modern morphology, but south central or western Asia are also possible. Unfortunately the Asian record from this period is limited, poorly known and insecurely dated.

Whatever the place and timing of modern human origins, modern groups clearly had some adaptive advantage over Neanderthals and other archaics, because these disappear from the fossil record. It is extremely difficult to know what this might have been: there appears to be nothing inherently advantageous in a slim, linear body build, reduced musculature, and globular braincase combined with flat face, weak jaws and overcrowded teeth. Nor is there any independent evidence of behavioural, technological or cognitive advance with the earliest anatomically moderns. In both sub-Saharan Africa and the Middle East their tool-kits and subsistence patterns are indistinguishable from Neanderthals and other archaics. There is thus no obvious and necessary link between the appearance of modern form and evidence for cognitive advance.

Nonetheless, around 45,000 years ago in the Middle East and 5-10,000 years later in Europe depending on region, the archaeological record reveals significant developments. Flake tools are replaced by blades - more economical of raw material, easier to transport and resharpen, and above all more specialised in form and function - together with a great expansion of bone, antler and ivory artefacts. Much of this is decorated, and by 30,000 in western Europe, there is evidence of rock art at Chauvet in the Ardeche. Evidence for mobile art in the form of decorated bone, antler and ivory, and of animal and human figures in these materials and in stone are known from even older sites across Europe. Particularly striking is the figure with a lion's head and a human body carved in mammoth ivory from Hohlenstein-stadel, south Germany, and dated to 30-33,000 years ago.

Transport networks were also extensive (high quality flint was regularly carried over distances of 100 -300 km and small, valued, items e.g. sea shells over much greater distances (200-500 km)), implying complex social contacts.

These and other items often appear to have been prized as decoration, and there is other evidence for body ornament. Burials were often covered in red ochre and may have spectacular numbers of decorative items such as beads, bracelets, pendants etc. as grave goods, pointing to economic surplus as personal 'wealth' and by inference, social differentiation.

All these indicators are associated with anatomically modern humans, but the pre-modern phase is not a black hole. For example, Neanderthals buried their dead, collected coloured pigments which show signs of being scraped or rubbed, also transported sea shells over sizeable distances, and latterly developed their own blade industries, presumably under the stimulus of contact with incoming moderns. But there is no definite evidence of Neanderthal grave goods, transported items are limited in quantity and shorter in range, and evidence for art and symbolism extremely scanty. The contrast between Neanderthal sites and the earliest European moderns (who, remember, are comparatively late compared with moderns elsewhere), is of a magnitude to make the divide effectively a qualitative one.

What underlies this explosion of the archaeological record? Many have suggested it reflects the development of full symbolic language, and some workers have attempted to argue that for anatomical reasons, Neanderthals could not produce the full range of sounds characteristic of modern human vocalisation. The evidence and arguments are decidedly shaky: vocalisation depends upon the configuration of the soft anatomy of the throat, which bears little relationship to the hard anatomy sometimes (if we are lucky) preserved via the fossil record. For what it is worth, the available evidence (not, in fact, very much - notably the delicate hyoid bone unusually preserved with a Neanderthal burial from Kebara, Israel) indicates a Neanderthal throat anatomy indistinguishable from that of modern humans.

Whatever, the details or underlying causes, it appears that some (not all) anatomically modern groups developed socio-cultural innovations that give them a reproductive edge over other groups, both modern and archaic, who lacked these and so subsequently disappeared. This need not have been via dramatic, direct confrontation and bloody genocide: computer modelling has shown that with two hunter gatherer groups in the same region, just a 1% reproductive advantage of one over the other will lead to the latter's marginalisation, displacement and disappearance within 1000 years. There is some evidence for this in the west European archaeological record: later Neanderthal sites in SW France are in peripheral, less optimal areas than the Dordogne, and southern Spain appears to have been a last relict area for them.

However, while some early modern groups developed these behavioural adaptations, there was no necessary and inevitable reason why they should have done so, and they could just as easily have been hit upon by Neanderthals who, after all, successfully occupied Europe for at least 100,000 years, and whose artefact assemblages shows them to have been responsive and adaptable. If that had happened, another twig of the hominid bush would show recent, luxuriant, growth and we would all look rather different. However, it was not so, and we bear witness to the actual evolutionary outcome. But it is an outcome heavily influenced by chance: contingency, not inevitability, produced the pattern that we are gradually uncovering from the archaeological, fossil and genetic evidence for human evolution.

Further Reading

Bilsborough, A., 1992. *Human Evolution,* Chapman & Hall

Conroy, G. C., 1997. *Reconstructing Human Origins,* Norton

Leakey, R. E. F., 1997. *The Origin of Humankind.* Weidenfeld & Nicolson

Mithen, S., 1996. *The Prehistory of Mind,* Thames & Hudson

Cultural Evolution - The Meme Hypothesis

Dr. Kate Distin

Philosophy Graduate and Trainee Teacher

"Most of what is unusual about man can be summed up in one word: 'culture'"[1]

Whilst it is contentious to claim that culture is humans' *only* distinguishing feature, nonetheless it seems clear that culture is one unique and fascinating aspect of our species. In this context, "culture" is not intended to be either a description of a narrow range of purely artistic pursuits, or a synonym for "society". "A *society* refers to an actual group of people and how they order their social relations. A *culture* ... refers to a body of socially transmitted information"[2]- the full spectrum of ideas, beliefs, skills, etc. that are available to us in society. It includes music, scientific theories, methods of transport, carpentry, literature, technology, art, clothing, mathematics, cartography, theatre, dry-stone-walling ... in short, the collective product of human activities and thought.

How did this body of knowledge and methods emerge? How does it now continue to develop? The hypothesis to be considered in this paper, is that culture is subject to some form of evolution. In order to test such a conjecture, though, it must first be decided which *sort* of evolutionary explanation is appropriate. Perhaps the most obvious answer, is that our cultural traits have evolved by just the same processes of natural selection as have all our other traits. The best available account of their development will, then, be ultimately biological - a specific application of Darwinism. An alternative, is that culture owes more to

---

1 Dawkins, 1989 p. 189

2 Barkhow, 1989 p. 118

nurture than to nature: that its evolution is an autonomous process, analogous to that in biology, but independent of it.

I turn first to the view that culture has evolved biologically.

Sociobiology

The name most immediately connected with the theory of evolution, is of course that of Charles Darwin. Since he believed that human behaviour can be attributed to just the same laws of descent as that of other species, it may be that sociobiology is the most appropriate means of studying human society. Sociobiology is "defined as the systematic study of the biological basis of all forms of social behaviour, in all kinds of organisms, including man."[3] Wilson does not claim exclusive control for our genes: he accepts that they interact with our cultural environment, during our development. Nonetheless, in response to the question to what *extent* human social behaviour is genetically determined, he replies that "The accumulated evidence for a large hereditary component is ... decisive."[4] In fact he goes even further, as can be seen in the following quotation:

"If the brain evolved by natural selection, even the capacities to select particular esthetic [*sic*] judgements and religious beliefs must have arisen by the same mechanistic process. They are either direct adaptations to past environments in which ancestral human populations evolved or at most constructions thrown up secondarily by deeper, less visible activities that were once adaptive in this stricter, biological sense."[5]

Cultural evolution, then, is forced along the paths permitted by genetic determinism: although some autonomy is allowed, there is a limit "beyond which biological evolution will begin

---

3 Wilson, 1978, p. 16

4 Wilson, 1978, p. 19

5 Wilson, 1978, p. 2

to pull cultural evolution back to itself"[6]; "cultures are not superorganisms that evolve by their own dynamics."[7]

Suggestions about how our biology might influence our culture are not limited to the mainstream sociobiologists: notoriously, Desmond Morris has labelled *Homo sapiens* "the naked ape"[8] and accounts for a vast range of present-day human behaviour by reference to ancient biological selection pressures. The chief problem with Morris's theory is that it does not in practice always remain true to his declared intent "largely to ignore the detailed ramifications of technology and verbalisation, and concentrate instead on those aspects of our lives that have obvious counterparts in other species"[9]. Rather, he quite frequently tries to explain specific features of particular cultures as the result of Darwinian selection, and fails to ask why - if such behaviour is the result of the human genotype - it is only found in that particular culture. Moreover, his explanations can appear to be distinctly *ad hoc* (e.g. his explanation[10] of the 'fact' that all people who eat alone in public feel uncomfortable: he claims that humans' carnivorous ancestry means that they are naturally inclined to make eating a social occasion; yet if people are uncomfortable in this situation, may it not simply be because they are alone in what is traditionally a meeting place? Would the same people really feel awkward about eating alone at home?).

Even when considering more mainstream sociobiology, we must be careful in our use of the term "genetically determined". Sociobiology assumes that genes are a more significant factor than the environment in controlling our

---

6 Wilson, 1978, p. 80

7 Wilson, 1978, p. 78

8 1968

9 1968, p. 11

10 BBC1, *The human animal*, 3rd August 1994

social behaviour, but this leaves open the question what *level* of social detail our genes control. There is nothing very interesting about the claim that broad, general aspects of social behaviour will, if advantageous, be selected: the whole point of society is to protect its members' genes and encourage their propagation, so behaviour or attitudes that tend to preserve social structures will (amongst social organisms) be favoured. On the other hand, this observation does not entail that specific, obscure features of society - its *cultural* facets - are genetically controlled. It is at least conceivable that the immense variation, amongst cultures, shows that many of the specific details are not genetically controlled.

On the other hand, sociobiologists may claim that "however it may work in detail, culture will usually enhance genetic fitness"[11] - and this does seem plausible, given the organic origin of the human capacity for culture. Trivial variations would not, if this were true, offer any challenge to the sociobiological hypothesis. So - is it a valid assertion? I think that it needs to be examined more closely, and should like to highlight three different ways in which it is open to misinterpretation.

Certainly, our *general* capacity for culture could not have evolved had it not initially been adaptively advantageous: the early development of the mind and of culture must have provided us with a mechanism to ensure that more of the successful cultural traits were beneficial than were harmful to us (because we still exist). It seems likely, in any case, that an advanced capacity for learning *would* have increased fitness[12]. My first point, though, is that this does not imply that each *particular* cultural trait will increase fitness.

---

11 Boyd and Richerson, 1985, p. 13

12 "In many circumstances the behaviour of experienced conspecifics is closer, on average, to the optimal behaviour

Secondly, the above assertion must also be distinguished from the claim that there will still, today, be a general correlation between cultural habits' popularity, and their helpfulness to us. Today the rate of cultural development is so great that most changes will be *neutral* with respect to our biological survival. There is an enormous disparity between modern culture and that of previous millennia, yet there is no reason to believe that the human brain of one, or even two thousand years ago was dissimilar to ours. This surely implies that the pace of cultural change is much too rapid to be picked up at the level of genes.

My third point also arises from the striking difference between the rates at which the physical and cultural worlds change. Think, for example, of the development of the computer, whose adaptive advantage is immeasurable - yet it would be ridiculous to assert that the human genetic code has changed to accommodate its understanding. This tells us that we must distinguish between the true fact that all human behaviour will fall within the potential range permitted by our genetic code, and the invalid deduction that where there is adaptive behaviour, there is always a genetic basis for it.

Clearly, none of the above undermines the claim that at least some of our cultural heritage is the product of our genes. What it does imply, is that sociobiology's application is more limited than its adherents maintain: it is relevant only to those cultural traits which are genetically determined. Sociobiology is simply a particular branch of the study of genes' effects - in this case, their effects on our culture. Thus it is inadequate to account for the *whole* of culture, since it appears that at least some culture is learnt rather than

---

than the behaviour that a naive individual could discover by itself. It imitation is also easier than trial-and-error learning, then it seems plausible that social learning would be favoured by selection." - Boyd and Richerson, 1985, p. 288

inherited (i.e. *any* branch of genetics is irrelevant to it). We shall therefore need another hypothesis, to account for the emergence and development of this portion of our culture. If we wish to stick with the evolutionary hypothesis, then perhaps it is more appropriate to bring it to bear on behaviour and the mind, than on neural architecture and its genetic code.

Of course, even the successful interpretation of such an hypothesis will leave unanswered the question *where* we should draw the line between genetic and environmental (i.e. cultural) control over behaviour. The closer this line is to the 'innate' extreme, the more significant will be the claims of sociobiology; the closer it is to the 'cultural' extreme, the less plausible they will be. I shall return to this issue at the end.

Cultural Evolution

The suggestion that evolution is not restricted to biology, but may also take place in the mental and cultural worlds, is appealing if hardly original. A metaphorical picture is often painted of ideas, theories, etc. 'evolving' through time, but can it ever justifiably be taken literally? That is, does Darwinism illustrate a process that can be applied to the mental and cultural at any level other than the fact that we, the subjects of minds and culture, are the products of biological descent? In order to answer this question, the consequences of the fundamental elements of evolutionary theory have to be worked out for the mental and cultural. The key problem is whether we can meaningfully apply to these areas the basic requirements for evolution: what would replication, variation or selection *be* in relation to mind and culture? Not until this has been explained, can we see whether there is genuine evolution of the mental and cultural.

Several writers, in recent years, have constructed models of how culture is transmitted and developed via social interaction. Amongst these are Cavalli-Sforza and Feldman (1981), Boyd and Richerson (1985), Barkhow (1989), Durham (1990 - he also quotes Lumsden and Wilson as a source). All refer to some sort of autonomous, cultural evolutionary process. Unfortunately there is not room, in this paper, to do justice to every variant of the cultural evolution hypothesis, so I have chosen to concentrate on just one: Richard Dawkins' "meme" theory.

There are several reasons for this focus. Firstly, *all* versions of a theory of cultural evolution are, for now at least, merely speculative. Thus it seems to me pointless to devote much time to their relative merits: better to use one model as an illustration, working on any inadequacies as necessary. Secondly, Dawkins himself has made some very strong claims about its theological significance, which it might be interesting to investigate. Thirdly, Dawkins' thesis is appealing because of its close analogy with neo-Darwinism: the mechanism it postulates for cultural evolution is simply a cultural analogue of the gene.

The Meme Hypothesis

Dawkins says that "Darwinism is too big a theory to be confined to the narrow context of the gene."[13] What is its *essential* feature? It is the differential survival of replicators - *any* replicators. Whatever the type of replicator involved, he conjectures, their variation under conditions of restricted resources would lead to a form of evolution.

In particular, he turns his attention to mental and cultural replicators (memes), for which he postulates a new form of selection, such that "once the genes have provided their survival machines with brains that are capable of rapid

---

13 1989, p. 191

imitation, the memes will automatically take over."[14] A meme is any "unit of information residing in a brain"[15]that is capable of replication; like a gene, it should be regarded as distinct from "its phenotypic effects, which are its consequences in the outside world"[16]. Thus it will, like a gene, be successful 'by proxy': via its phenotypic effects (the external consequences of that piece of information). Words, skills, and music are "the outward and visible (audible, etc.) manifestations of the memes within the brain"[17], which are transmitted between individuals via their sense organs, leaving on the recipient's brain a (not necessarily exact) copy that is free to transmit again.

As examples of memes, Dawkins suggests ideas, catch-phrases, tunes (or snatches of tunes), fashions and skills. As with genes, the constituents of success will be long life, fecundity and accuracy of replication. The element of competition necessary for any selection to take place is introduced by the brain's limited attention: in order to dominate, a meme must distract the brain's attention from other memes. Success in this matter will depend upon the structure of the brain, as well as on the stability of the meme and its "penetrance in the cultural environment"[18]. The latter will depend on psychological appeal, and according to Dawkins this means (as for genes) that co-adapted complexes - i.e. evolutionarily stable sets of memes - will occur. Selection will favour those memes capable of exploiting the current cultural environment, which obviously includes other memes also trying to be selected. As sets of memes co-operate, new ones will find it more difficult to

---

14 1989, p. 200

15 Dawkins, 1982, p.109

16 *Ibid*

17 1982, p. 109

18 1989, p. 193

penetrate the environment later: the complex provides protection against invasion. Particularly in areas such as theories of science will the compatibility rule apply. For other types of memes different criteria will apply - 'catchiness' for tunes, for example.

Dawkins emphasises that memes' success will *not* depend on the (dis)advantages they produce for the genotypes that gave rise to the brains they inhabit. Memes, like genes, are selfish: their success depends on the advantages that they confer on *themselves*. In the struggle for brains' attention, they must in some way be 'better' than their rivals, but this need have nothing to do with the effects that they have on their possessors' genes' success. "Selection favours memes that exploit their cultural environment to their own advantage."[19] Although the needs of genes and memes may often coincide (a meme will not last long if causes its possessor to die before he can transmit it, for example), they may sometimes be in complete opposition: Dawkins uses the example of a meme for celibacy to illustrate this possibility.

The Gene-Meme Analogy

Notice that, although 'memetic' evolution may for convenience be referred to as 'analogous to' genetic evolution, this should not be taken to imply that the former is theoretically dependent on the latter. Whilst it is true that in the chronological order of theoretical development, memetic evolution has been inspired by the theory of genetic evolution, this is not the order of explanatory dependence. Rather, both are examples of a more abstract, generally applicable theory of the evolution of replicators under conditions of competition.

In fact the use of the term 'analogy', in this context, deserves closer attention. Usually this term implies that at

---

[19] Dawkins, 1989, p. 199

least one side of the comparison is fairly well developed - we talk about electric 'current', for instance, because water flow is familiar to us - and an analogy would not be of any use if this were not the case. Another sort of scientific comparison, however, is exemplified by gravitational and electrostatic forces, where a new student can easily see the similarity between Newton's law of universal gravitation:

"The force between two masses is directly proportional to the product of their masses and inversely proportional to the square of their separation."

and Coulomb's law:

"The force between two point charges is directly proportional to the product of their charges and inversely proportional to the square of their separation."

without being familiar with either field. The relationship between memetics and genetics is best understood as a combination of these alternatives. A meme (if it exists at all) is not, strictly speaking, an analogue of a gene: rather it is a different token of the same type of entity, a replicator. Similarly, mental evolution is (if true) a different example of the same type of process as neo-Darwinism, rather than a simple analogue of it. The two processes have the same description at a sufficiently functional, abstract level. Nonetheless, because we are already familiar with genetics, we can use it to illuminate memetics.

In summary: although we should not expect the particular details of biological evolution to carry over into mental evolution, it seems reasonable to exploit our knowledge of neo-Darwinism as a guide to what the essential elements of mental evolution might be. This sort of comparison between two phenomena is far from unique in science, where it is quite common to find different tokens of the same type of process realised within different media (c.f. the fact that wave properties such as diffraction, interference, refraction, etc. may all be observed in water waves as well as in electromagnetic and sound waves). As Darden and Cain point out, "comparison of two examples is a good way to locate what is most important", and helps in "pruning away content and leaving essentials"[20].

Support For The Meme Hypothesis

Having clarified the nature of its relationship to genetics, the question remains why (if at all) we should accept the meme hypothesis.

For Darwin, the starting point of his line of thought about natural selection, was that variations occur within the traits of a species. Variation seems to be a good starting place for a theory of mental evolution, too. There are often marked differences amongst the beliefs and practices of those who would claim to have the same concept, skill or idea, and it is possible to trace the extent of such variation to the point where two people at either extreme of it would deny that they have the same idea at all. Two people who share what might loosely be called the "same" skill, of piano-playing, may more accurately be classified into two separate categories: concert pianists and jazz improvisers, for example. Two people who share what might loosely be called the same life-style and set of beliefs, and both call themselves Christians, may more appropriately be referred to as Greek Orthodox and Methodist. In other words, it seems fairly uncontentious to note that there is variation within those aspects of our mental and cultural life that might be regarded as memes.

How might memetic variations occur? For genes, mutation is perhaps the most obvious factor in the production of variation, but in fact the more frequent means of variation is recombination. Although it would not be appropriate to try

---

20 1989, p. 109

to extrapolate from the detailed structural ways in which genetic variation occurs, to the ways in which memetic variation might occur, still it might be useful to discuss the nature of (and limitations on) this aspect of evolution as applied to genes. Such a discussion should illuminate the significant elements of the variation that is necessary for evolution.

One of the most significant features of genetic variation, is that there are limits on the 'innovation' to which it can give rise. There are obvious limitations on possible recombinations, in that alleles[21] have to correspond and the possible recombinations are, though rich, finite with respect to any given gene pool. Popularly, however, genetic mutation is referred to as 'random' and, unless used with care, this term may easily lead to confusion - it certainly does not mean that all genetic changes are equally likely. 'Random' is a context-dependent term, used to indicate that its subject is free from a specific form of causal control. If it is used independently of that context, i.e. without specifying from which kind of control a process is free, then the term becomes confusing and perhaps even meaningless. The important sense in which genetic mutation *is* random, is that it entails "no general bias towards bodily improvement"[22] (rather, most mutation is probably fatal). Evolution's tendency towards improvement stems solely from natural selection.

What are the implications for memes, of this brief discussion of genetic mutation?[23] I think it clear that in the cultural

21 Editors Note: An allele is one form of a gene.

22 Dawkins, 1986, p. 307

23 In the absence of any other immediate candidates for the same rôle, the study of mutation and recombination will provide a useful springboard for the investigation of memetic variation.

realm, too, there are changes that might realistically be characterised as "mutations": unpredictable alterations in existing concepts, practices and ideas. Such changes, too, seem to be random with respect to their own fitness - equally likely to be altered in a way that makes them less successful in their field, as to be improved by the mutation. Think of a mistake or experiment during cooking - are you really any more likely to make a change for the better, than for the worse? Similarly a mistake during a scientific experiment, a wrong note during a music recital, or a miscopied part of a text or poem seems to me to be, if anything, *more* likely to be a "one-off", never repeated, than it does to be a resounding and much-replicated success.

I think that there are also cultural events that might be described as "recombinations" - and that they, too, are subject to restrictions analogous to those in the biological world (i.e. "alleles" have to "match"). Rather than novelties, these are instances in which one existing method, idea, theory, etc. is replaced with another that already exists: the Church congregation is accompanied by a guitar rather than an organ, for instance. In such cases, the replacement concept has to control the same cultural feature as its predecessor: you could replace a dry-stone wall with a hedge but not with a bungalow; and you could replace a bungalow with a terraced house but not with a hedge; you could sing "While shepherds washed their socks by night" in the place of "While shepherds watched their flocks by night", but not in the place of "All seated on the ground".

Arguably, then, memetic variations occur and can be explained along lines similar to those in genes. Are they passed on to offspring? Clearly, 'offspring' does not here refer to biological but to cultural descendants - and it seems obvious that the variations *are* transmitted, in this sense. If my piano teacher is a concert pianist then he will teach me to read music, with an emphasis on the repetitive practice of pieces that I have first sight-read; if he is a jazz pianist then he will teach me the techniques of improvisation, and how to play by ear. If my Philosophy tutor subscribes to a particular brand of Dualism then my reading may be directed towards Descartes, whereas if he is a Behaviourist then he might suggest Ryle. This does not, of course, guarantee that I will eventually decide to be Cartesian or Behaviourist myself (apart from anything else, I will have many more cognitive than genetic 'parents'), but it *does* guarantee that I will *learn* about those theories. Just as the variations that you inherit from a biological parent may develop differently in you, depending on the nature of your environment and the genes that you inherited from your other parent, so the variations that you acquire from your cultural predecessors (who might be your teachers, people whose books you have read, musicians whose style you have imitated, etc.) may develop differently in the context of your mind and environment. What matters from the point of view of evolution, however, is that those variations *are* replicated in you.

Meme theory, then, depends on the existence of a mechanism for the replication of cultural information. There are two aspects to any form of replication: the information that is copied, and its means of transmission. Genes, for instance, preserve (in DNA) the information needed to control a certain phenotypic effect, from one generation to the next; this information is replicated, of course, via various forms of biological reproduction. Memes, too, must in some way be able to preserve and copy information, between 'generations'. Memes must be *about* (rather than identical with) the things that they affect: a mandolin, for instance, is not also a meme 'for' a mandolin - rather, it is the external effect which that meme controls. Perhaps the best way to describe a meme, is as a concept. As such, it will be preserved in whichever form is most appropriate: memory-based, linguistic, diagrammatic, symbolic, artistic, etc.

In order to replicate, memes need also to be able to pass on the information that they preserve in such forms. I think that there is little controversial about the claim that concepts are continually being transmitted. Methods involved might be intentional (formal pedagogy, or normal conversation), or they might be almost unconscious - as when one person simply imitates another's actions or reads about their ideas. As with the analogous process of gene transmission, the resultant copies will not always be exact, and the idea or skill in question may change in some way *en route*. The essence of any such process, however, is that it imparts the representational content of the relevant idea, theory, skill, etc. It will be apparent that the novel meme has been acquired, when its external consequences are displayed by the recipient: when he applies it in practice, or is able to pass it on by explaining it to someone else. This point also highlights the fact that what has been taught, told or imitated is a generally applicable method or concept, etc., rather than particular solutions or explanations. The particular solutions are rather the *effects* of having acquired the general method.

In culture as in biology, then, variations exist and are passed on to the next 'generation'. The next strand in Darwin's argument came from Malthus's theory of a population which increases much faster than its limited resources. From this, Darwin extracted the idea of the struggle for existence, which is as important a structural feature of evolutionary theory as is variation. Is it true that the mental and cultural 'population' also increases at a swifter rate than its resources?

The answer to this must depend on the definitions of a mental and cultural 'population', and of the nature of its 'resources'. The contenders for membership of the mental and cultural population seem innumerable: ideas, concepts, skills, concertos, fashions, ways of building houses, farming methods, ... These all seem to be aspects of the mental and cultural (traditions, thoughts, etc.) that might potentially be passed on from one possessor of them to another. Meme theory needs some sort of criterion of memetic 'fitness' - something that all these ideas, skills, etc. have in common, in virtue of which their relative success rates can be subject to systematic study - for without this it breaks down into the trivial statement that out of many new ideas, skills, etc., some survive whilst others do not.

The general fitness criterion for genes - the question what will influence their chances of survival and reproduction - is the influence they have on their bearer's ability to find food and sex. So what is the general fitness criterion for the mental or cultural population? It seems clear that the memetic population's 'resource' is the limited attention of human brains, and therefore that a given meme's (or meme-complex's) fitness, or chances of survival and reproduction, will be influenced chiefly by its ability to gain and retain its bearers' attention: gaining someone's attention is a means of replicating itself (c.f. sex), and retaining that attention is a means of prolonging its survival (c.f. food).

Beyond this very general memetic fitness criterion of attention gain and retention, however, the factor that determines memes' fitness levels will vary widely between contexts: whether or not a meme is successful will depend on a variety of fitness criteria, determined by the area of culture to which it pertains. The same is true in biology - to give a crude example, genes that produce giraffe-type necks will not benefit an elephant. The 'particular' question about fitness is therefore how an individual meme, given the demands of its environment, can ensure greater access to its means of reproduction and survival (i.e. gaining and retaining attention). Since memes, like genes, are selected by proxy, this question must be answered in terms of the interaction between the environment and the meme's phenotypic effects. If the effect is a scientific theory then it must enjoy some degree of explanatory success, must not contradict existing theories but must also accord with the available perceptual evidence; if it is a melody or a picture then it must be aesthetically pleasing, and the conditions that this entails may be determined temporally or geographically; if it is a recipe then it must result in good tasting, non-toxic things to eat, and again decisions about the former may differ between cultures.

More generally, factors such as: compatibility with existing memes; the commitment with which they are held; empirical evidence; any evangelical element of a concept - will also come into play. The main point is that, in order to maintain some sort of grip on day-to-day reality, we have to choose between the skills, theories, etc. on which we might focus our efforts and keep available in memory. Thus it appears that the mental and cultural population does increase faster than its resources.

From the transmission of variations and the struggle for existence, Darwin derived natural selection: in the struggle for the resources of a limited environment, those organisms with slightly advantageous variations will have a better chance of survival and replication, whereas those whose variations are at all deleterious will find their survival threatened. There is no great difficulty for mental evolution with this stage of Darwin's argument, for it consists merely in deducing the consequences of the previous stages (though, as noted above, those consequences will be played out at a far greater pace than is the case in biology). A form of selection must occur in minds and culture, and we should expect to see the preservation of those ideas, skills, etc. with the best fit to their environment, and the extinction of those without.

Finally, in order to move his theory from adaptation by natural selection to a genuine account of the emergence of new species, Darwin invoked two new principles: divergence, and geographical isolation. Present day theories of speciation are not restricted to these two principles, and (so far as I can gather) there is no consensus on which theory is correct. What matters about any such theory, though, is that it attempts to provide an explanation of how variations can become so great that they produce new species. The question thus arises whether such an explanation is available or even appropriate for a theory of mental and cultural evolution. Its answer must depend on what in that theory, if anything, will correspond to the species in biology[24].

Recall that mental and cultural evolution can be expected to share the significant structural features of Darwinism, but not its specific details (since it is not a straightforward analogue of Darwinism, but a process of the same type that Darwinism illustrates). Speciation is, I think, a detail rather than a structural feature: it is a side effect of biological evolution, and is not intrinsic to its operation in the way that variation or selection is. It so happens that, in the natural world, organisms have diversified to the extent that we can now categorise them into separate species, but I do not think that it will be appropriate to seek the equivalent in the mental world. It may be that we can treat, say, different

---

24 A species is "a group of individuals of common ancestry which closely resemble each other structurally and physiologically and, in nature, interbreed, producing fertile offspring" (Steen, 1971, p. 513)

cultures as the 'analogues' of different species, but this issue is, I think, peripheral.[25]

Memes and mental viruses

Having offered a brief defence and development of the meme hypothesis, I should like to emphasise, once again, how much care needs to be taken with the gene-meme analogy. Ironically, the example that I use to illustrate the errors that can arise by taking the analogy too literally, stems from the originator of meme theory.

Dawkins speculates about the extent to which a certain type of cultural replicator might be seen more as the analogue of a virus than of a gene. As an example of this sort of replicator he uses religion, and concludes that it "is best understood as an infectious disease of the mind"[26]. This analysis he uses to add weight to his already well-publicised conviction that truth is incompatible with religion. The aim of the remainder of this section is to discover whether his arguments constitute a valid application of meme theory.

Dawkins starts with a discussion of the nature of physical viruses, and describes them simply as "Duplicate Me" programs written in the language of the DNA code. Their advent was "inevitable" once the cellular machinery for DNA replication had developed, for such an apparatus provides the perfect niche for "subversive, parasitic 'Duplicate Me' programs"[27], which hijack genes' replicative machinery in order to make copies of themselves.

---

25 If I am wrong, and speciation is a structural feature of biological evolution, then the emergence of separate categories of meme-complexes will deserve more attention. At this point, however, I see no benefits in pursuing this line of enquiry

26 1993b

27 1993b

Thus Dawkins contrasts viral with genetic methods of survival. Both use the same means of replication, but genes produce it and viruses hijack it: genes' replicative success depends on their producing beneficial effects on their possessors' chances of survival and reproduction, whereas viruses' replicative success depends merely on their ensuring that they are replicated. (C.f. the fact that a robin's successful procreation depends on its *providing* a safe environment for its chicks, in which they are continually fed; a cuckoo's depends merely on ensuring that its chicks *enter* such an environment.) Turning to non-biological parasites, he says that our brains, with their naturally selected openness to memes, also provide an environment that is ripe for exploitation.

I think that it will be helpful for me to clarify (my interpretation of) some of the finer points of his analogy, before looking further into his arguments. If we accept the meme hypothesis, then in what way should we expect 'mental viruses' to differ from memes? To uphold the biological analogy, we should expect mental viruses to succeed by parasitising the replicative machinery of teaching, imitation and communication, in order to make copies of themselves. There must be a normal process of replication, upon which such viruses are parasitic. We should expect the sorts of ideas, etc. that are viral rather than memetic to be taught and imitated not because of any replicative advantage they hold over other ideas (are better predictors, more aesthetically pleasing, etc.), but merely because they have found some way of ensuring that they are taught and imitated. Putting this another way, the viral nature of a replicator is dependent on its method of replication rather than on its content. With this criterion in mind, I return now to Dawkins' argument.

He begins by explaining the properties that make a medium vulnerable to parasitic exploitation: its (almost) accurate replicative powers, and a willingness to obey the instructions that it is replicating. The human brain, he argues, has just these properties. He points out that, in addition, the mind of a child is especially susceptible to parasitic exploitation: it *needs* to be receptive to new ideas, in order to soak up a whole culture and language. In this context, Dawkins first introduces the idea that religion is just such a virus of the mind, able to manipulate the thought processes of its victim - although the victim will be unaware of being so manipulated.

Dawkins contrasts such 'viruses' with 'good' memes. He says that we should be careful not to apply the viral analogy to all ideas and all aspects of culture: some are more like "good genes" than self-serving, "Duplicate Me" viruses. Indeed, "great ideas and great music spread, not because they embody instructions, slavishly carried out, but because they are great. The works of Darwin and Bach are not viruses."[28] Equally, although scientific ideas might seem to spread epidemiologically, in fact they spread "because people evaluate them, recommend them and pass them on"[29].

In such statements, Dawkins comes perilously close to labelling only those things of which *he* approves, as "great" and non-viral. Indeed, I should like to claim that his meme/virus distinction displays a misunderstanding of his own theory. In *The Selfish Gene*, he said that "selection favours memes that exploit their cultural environment to their own advantage"[30]. Yet if this is the case, then how can the difference between good memes and mental viruses rest on the question whether the replicator in question is a 'good'

---

28 1993b

29 1993a, p. 26

30 p. 199

one? We cannot just dismiss as "viral" those ideas whose content we see as harmful or pointless. Even for genes, it is not relevant that (usually) the virus is bad and the gene good for the individual who acquires it: both are replicators, and the distinction between them is a developmental one.

Dawkins' confusion is apparent throughout his discussion of memes and viruses. Contrast, for example, his claim that "the selective forces that scrutinise scientific ideas are not arbitrary or capricious ... they do not favour pointless self-serving behaviour"[31], with his characterisation of memes as having "no foresight. They are unconscious, blind, replicators"[32].

He also seems, in his discussion of mental viruses, to have misinterpreted the very essence of the gene-meme comparison. A detail-to-detail analogy is not appropriate between genetics and memetics. In an endnote to the earliest edition of *The Selfish Gene*, Dawkins states that he wants "to claim almost limitless power for slightly inaccurate self-replicating entities, once they arise anywhere in the universe". In proposing his meme theory, he was "trying to make the case for replicators in general, and to show that genes were not the only members of that important class"[33]. From quotations such as these it is clear that Dawkins intended the comparisons between genes and memes to be made at a very general, structural level. The meme hypothesis loses much of its credibility as soon as one tries to claim that every feature of genetics can be carried over to the mental. Why on earth should this be possible? The point of the meme hypothesis was that if the essential features of Darwinism can be found in the mental and cultural worlds, then we should expect to see a new type of evolution taking

---

31 1993a, p. 26

32 1989, p. 200

33 p. 322

place in those media. The specifics of how the new type of evolution will develop, however, need not parallel those of its predecessor, biological evolution. I think it obvious that viruses, as parasites on the biological evolutionary system, are not essential features of it.

If, on the other hand, Dawkins wishes merely to claim that religious beliefs spread memetically, then this will say *nothing* about the truth value of their subject matter. It will show merely that religious beliefs do not, as scientists and philosophers so often claim, have to be held at the expense of one's intellect. Memetics, like genetics, is merely an hypothesis about the transmission and development of information. Although both theories account for the relation between that information and its external consequences, neither has anything to say about its intrinsic value. Biological fitness is a relative concept: genetic variation *a* may be selected rather than *b*, but this does not tell us whether *a* is 'really' an efficient method of survival and propagation. For the answer to that question, we have to appeal to theories other than neo-Darwinism (engineering, for instance). Similarly, if idea *x* is selected rather than *y*, this tells us nothing about the truth, elegance or any other value of *x*. For that information, we have to appeal to other theories (aesthetics, for instance, or truth criteria). Thus, if religion does spread and evolve memetically, the question of its validity is as open as ever.

Memes vs. genes

The final question to which I turn, may be asked whether or not the meme hypothesis is accepted. It is the perennial puzzle of where we should draw the line between "nature" and "nurture": to what extent are we the product of biological evolution, and to what extent are we influenced by our culture? In terms of memetics, this may be rephrased in terms of the relative influences of genes and memes, but I think that this discussion could meaningfully be transposed into one that did not contain the word "meme" at all, for those who are still uncomfortable with it.

I think it obvious that neither factor is wholly responsible for us: genes without environmental input (nourishment, etc.) are useless; culture without genes is non-existent. Nonetheless, the question remains which is the *most* significant factor, and in order to formulate some sort of answer to this, I shall appeal to what Sober[34] calls the "positive main effect", a concept that can be used in answering the following question: given a trait that varies within a population, is biology or the environment the main influence on its variation?

Genes exert a positive main effect on a trait, if an alteration in the population's genotype causes a change in the average phenotype, with respect to that trait. The environment exerts a positive main effect, if a difference in it causes a change in the average phenotype, with respect to the trait in question. The major influence on that trait's variation, within the population, is that which exerts the greater main effect. An example[35] may help to clarify these concepts. Consider the question whether genotype or environment is the major influence on humans' ability to use natural language. Since this trait is universal amongst humans, we need to embed humans within a larger population, in order to see whether genetic differences have any effect. In which circumstances is the language ability developed?

---

34 1993, ch. 7

35 Based on Sober, 1993, p. 190. Notice that, in both this example and the following one (my own), the accuracy of the (purely speculative) tabled results is not the issue - the point is merely to elucidate the concepts involved.

	Exposed to a human language	Not exposed to a human language
Human genes	Yes	No
Chicken genes	No	No

If this table displays accurate results, then it shows that the biological and environmental influences on language acquisition are equal: the right genes are necessary, but so is the right environment. For another example - perhaps a belief in God - the results may be different:

	Exposed to an organised religion	Not exposed to an organised religion
Human genes	Sometimes	Sometimes (less often)
Chicken genes	Never	Never

If *this* table's results are realistic, then it shows that the genetic influences on Theism are greater than the cultural ones - even though there *is* a degree of cultural effect. Without the right genes, the belief will never be acquired, but without the ideal environment it still might be.

Now, it seems to me obvious that genes will exert the major (or, at the very least, an equal) influence over most social traits that are both unique to and universal amongst human beings. In fact, this is almost a truism: if you are not human, then you cannot have uniquely human traits, and if you are human then you are bound to have the universal ones. For these traits, then, sociobiology will be able to offer the best account. Social traits that are universal amongst, but not unique to humans will be best explained by the genetic differences between those species that share the traits in question (e.g. primates), and those that do not.

It is when we consider traits that are unique to, but not universal amongst humans, that the controversy arises.

I would argue that cultural evolution can offer a better account of these, than can Darwinism. Traits that vary amongst cultures must, if genes are to be cited as their major influence, correlate with genetic differences between the populations concerned. In the sorts of specific cases to which I have referred, throughout this paper, I think that this is implausible. Is sociobiology really going to claim that every person who uses self-raising flour in pastry, plays Jazz rather than Classical piano, prays through Icons rather than directly, or whatever, shares certain genetic characteristics which are lacking in those who do not?

Of course it is not - to argue against this sort of view, is to challenge a straw man - but Wilson *would* argue that all human institutions "evolve in directions that enhance the welfare of the practitioners"[36]. In other words, there is a sufficiently broad category, from which these specific variations have grown, that *does* have genes as its major influence. In the cases above, these areas might for instance be cookery, music and religious practice. My argument, however, is that such categories are general enough to be universal amongst, as well as unique to humans - and that, as such, it is not surprising that they are explicable by Darwinism. On the other hand, the evolution of *non*-universal traits within these categories is not primarily the result of genetic differences, and is therefore *in*explicable by Darwinism.

It is not even necessary to phrase this conclusion in terms of the controversial meme theory. We simply need to say that if social learning, rather than genetic inheritance, is the major influence in the development of a cultural trait, then it is inappropriate to try to explain that trait as a result of biological evolution; this is true despite the fact that, as sociobiologists emphasise, we are ultimately genetic

---

[36] 1978, p. 175

creatures. The challenge that the meme hypothesis *does* present to those who dismiss it, is to find a better account of the development and complexity of those aspects of human culture which are not subject to biological evolution.

References

BARKHOW, JEREMY H. (1989): *The elastic between genes and culture*, Ethology and Sociobiology 10, 111-26

BOYD, R. & RICHERSON, P. J. (1985): *Culture and the evolutionary process*, Chicago University Press

CAVALLI-SFORZA, L. L. & FELDMAN, M. (1981): *Cultural transmission and evolution: a quantitative approach*, Princeton University Press

DARDEN, C. & CAIN, J. A. (1989): *Selection type theories*, Philosophy of Science 56, 106-29

DAWKINS, RICHARD (1982): *The extended phenotype*, Oxford University Press

DAWKINS, RICHARD (1989 edition): *The selfish gene*, Oxford University Press

DAWKINS, RICHARD (1993a): *Viruses of the mind* (pp. 13-27 of Dahlbom 1993), Blackwell

DAWKINS, RICHARD (1993b): *Is religion just a disease?*, The Daily Telegraph, 15/12/93, p. 18

DURHAM (1990): *Advances in evolutionary culture theory*, Annual Review of Anthropology 19, 187-210

MORRIS, DESMOND (1968): *The naked ape*, Corgi

RUSE, MICHAEL (1989): *Philosophy of biology*, MacMillan

SOBER, ELLIOTT (1993): *Philosophy of biology*, Oxford University Press

STEEN, E. B. (1971): *Dictionary of biology*, Barnes and Noble

WILSON, E. O. (1978), *On human nature*, Penguin

The Evolution of Language; Truth and Lies

Professor Stephen R.L. Clark

Dean of Arts Faculty, Liverpool University

How is Language Possible?

Books on the origins of language usually include Herodotus's anecdote about Psamtik I, of Egypt: Psamtik, wishing to discover the first language of humanity, arranged for two children to be reared upon an island, by deaf-mutes, and their first words recorded. When they gave voice to a word identifiable as the Phrygian term for bread, it was decided that Phrygian must be the one original tongue. The experiment has been repeated since, at least in imagination, and the original identified as Hebrew, Sanskrit, French or what you will.

The story is told, of course, to mock the enterprise. The authors of these books believe that children reared like that would never talk at all: we have the evidence of feral, and of seriously neglected children, to convince us that we must be exposed to language at a critical age if we are ever to manage more than the stumbling phrases of one such victim: 'Mike paint. Applesauce buy store. Neal come happy. Neal not come sad' (Pinker p.292). Nothing that such children produce of themselves is much like a language, let alone the One Original which custom has distorted.

Oddly enough, rather few authors draw the puzzling conclusion: that no-one can ever have learned a language. There is no point speaking if no-one understands. Indeed, there is probably no *chance* of speaking if no-one understands (since there is no-one to confirm or disconfirm one's usage). Nor is there any need to speak, even to oneself. And, as a matter of fact, children do not speak if no-one speaks around them - but in that case, who spoke first, and why? James Beattie, writing in 1788: 'If there was a time when all mankind were a dumb and brutal race of animals, all mankind must, in the ordinary course of events, have continued dumb to this day. For first, to such animals speech could not be necessary; as they are supposed to have existed for ages without it; and it is not to be imagined, that dumb and beastly savages would ever think of contriving unnecessary arts, whereof they had no example in the world around them' (cited by Hattiangadi p.171; see Kenny).

No one without words can have 'invented' them. Lucretius, recording Epicurean opinion: 'To think that someone in those days assigned names to things, and that is how men learnt their first words, is crazy. Why should he have been able to indicate all things with sounds, and to utter the various noises of the tongue, yet others be supposed not to have had that ability at the same time? Besides, if others had not already used sounds to each other, how did he get the preconception of their usefulness implanted in him? How did he get the initial capacity to know and see with his mind what he wanted to do?' (5.1040ff, in Long & Sedley 19B: I, pp.97f). The Epicureans explained human speech by suggesting that our ancestors produced relevant gestures and sounds by nature, and that local circumstances (and later history) generated all the different tongues (Long & Sedley 19A, 19B). It may be that there is some truth in this, but it is open to the obvious retort that human tongues, unlike the communication systems of other animals, employ arbitrary, conventional signs which refer to things that are not around, and may not exist at all. Augustine, drawing on Stoic argument: 'Some signs are natural, others given. Natural signs are those which without a wish or any urge to signify cause something else besides themselves to be known from them, like smoke, which signifies fire. ... The expression of an angry or depressed person signifies an emotional state even if there is no such wish on the part of the person who is angry or depressed. ... Given signs are those which living things give to each other, in order to show, to the best of their ability, the emotions of their minds, or anything they have felt or learnt. ... Some animals too have signs among themselves by which they show the desire of their minds: a cockerel on finding food gives a vocal sign to its hen to come quickly, and a dove calls to, or is called by, its mate by cooing. ... Whether (as with a facial expression or a shout of pain) they accompany emotion without any desire to signify, or whether they are really given in order to signify something, is another question' (De DC 2.3: p.58f) - which is still not answered. And again: 'All these meanings [of Greek and Latin homophones like *lege*] derive their effect on the mind from each individual's agreement with a particular convention. As this agreement varies so does the effect. People did not agree to use them because they were already meaningful: rather they became meaningful because people agreed to use them' (De DC 2.95: p.101). And how could they have made the first agreements?

Sextus Empiricus, arguing against the theoreticians of his day, made the issue clear: on the one hand, there are no merely 'natural' languages, instantly accessible to humans of whatever place or time, and on the other, no-one can *agree* to use one set of merely conventional rules, or merely conventional terms, without already sharing such conventions (see Glidden p.143). Augustine himself recognised part of the problem: we cannot show anyone what even such a simple term as 'walking' means by mere ostension. 'How am I to guard against his thinking that it is just the amount of walking I have done?' (De Magistro

10.29: see Kirwan p.206). There are gestures (like pointing) which strike us as obvious: surely it would be easy enough to *indicate* (which is, to point) what object went with what sign? But there are no objects with entirely obvious boundaries (as Quine's *gavagai* makes clear[1]), and pointing itself is a convention: interestingly, deaf children learning to sign 'used the sign of pointing to their conversation partners to mean "me" at exactly the age at which hearing children use the sound *you* to mean "me". The children were treating the gesture as a pure linguistic symbol: the fact that it pointed somewhere did not register as being relevant.' (Pinker p.152) There are some gestures found throughout the species, with some similar effects (smiles, frowns, widened eyes and lifted eyebrows, for example), but even these are assigned different conventional values (Crystal p.402). Whether we beckon with palm up or down, or assent by nodding our heads up or down, are as conventional as saying 'Come'.

The puzzle would be made still greater if, as Stoics argued (and innumerable sages since have variously repeated), there could be no thoughts at all until they can be spoken. If no-one can identify any event or object till they have a word for it (and follow the public rules for using just that word), how can they possibly acquire the knowledge? What must this be but magic, or a miracle?

---

[1] Quine imagines a tribe whose single exclamation 'gavagai!' is visibly associated with the presence of, as we would say, a rabbit: since it is also, and inevitably, associated with the presence of rabbit-meat or temporal slices of a rabbit life, we cannot learn the meaning of the term merely by ostension.

CHRIST & THE COSMOS XI

They do not live in the world,
Are not in time and space.
From birth to death hurled
No word do they have, not one
To plant a foot upon,
Were never in any place.

For with names the world was called
Out of the empty air,
With names was built and walled,
Line and circle and square,
Dust and emerald;
Snatched from deceiving death
By the articulate breath.

But these have never trod
Twice the familiar track,
Never never turned back
Into the memoried day.
All is new and near
In the unchanging Here
Of the fifth great day of God,
That shall remain the same,
Never shall pass away.

On the sixth day we came.
('The Animals': Muir p.207)

Muir's metaphor, however moving, is inaccurate: the animals he has in mind were also created, so the story says, on the sixth day (and Biblical writers have no doubt that animals think and feel). That story makes better sense than Stoic theory. 'The discussions that assume that language determines thought carry on only by a collective suspension of disbelief. A dog, Bertrand Russell notes, may not be able to tell you that its parents were honest though poor, but can anyone really conclude from this that the dog is *unconscious*'(Pinker p.58). Apparently they can, sometimes adding that human infants are unconscious too. That is not a claim that I am willing to discuss. But there remains a puzzle: what sort of consciousness preceded human language, and how could anything with such a consciousness have ever 'agreed' to the conventions necessary for speech?

In brief, there are very few entirely 'natural' signs incorporated in any human tongue, and even those which once were natural may have been given new meanings. So feral or neglected children have no 'natural' tongue, nor any way of acquiring competence in a conventional. And since our ancestors, presumably, were once such feral children, they did not learn to speak, and nor have their descendants.

Which is of course, as Beattie knew, absurd. So what has happened?

The Irrelevance of Mere Intelligence

Science fiction writers, mostly for the sake of a good story, prefer to suggest that evolutionary changes are bound to favour the emergence of humanoid intelligence and language. SETI enthusiasts make the same assumption. Unfortunately, most creatures throughout terrestrial history have managed very well without intelligence, and without language. Even though some creatures have profited by being quick to adapt means to ends and to communicate dangers or opportunities or invitations to their conspecifics, none - except ourselves - have ever (as far as we know) developed the sort of global understanding or linguistic capability we hope to identify *Out There*. Eyes have evolved independently, it seems, on forty or more separate occasions during terrestrial evolution: human intelligence just once. Biologists - unlike astronomers - do not generally expect to discover creatures any more intelligent than bees or squirrels *Out There*, and would be almost as surprised to be proved wrong as to discover that the aliens had invented English. English is the unpredictable product of immensely many accidents. Once it exists, as a global lingua franca, there is undoubtedly a great advantage to be had by learning it, but there would be no particular advantage to a solitary speaker, nor any reason to expect it to emerge all at once. Human language itself may turn out to be just such an accidental accumulation of words and rules: why should any creature anywhere begin to develop it? And even if there were some parallel developments, would they add up to any language *we* could learn? If God is indeed what theists[2] have supposed, there may indeed be a far greater chance of humanoid intelligence on other worlds: and the discovery of such extraterrestrial intelligence would therefore be evidence for theism!

It is easy to fall back on common sense. After all, some say, it is surely 'obvious' that animals would gain by being able to gather information about their environment, and share it with their relatives - as bees do. There might also be reasons *not* to share the information: a young chimpanzee who hoots

---

[2] Theism is the belief in a personal God as creator and supreme ruler of the universe, who transcends his creation but works in and through it, thus revealing himself, as opposed to Deism which is the belief in the existence of a personal God who created the universe, set it in motion, subject to natural laws but takes no part in its running. (Editor's note)

at the discovery of food will probably lose the food (and will probably not make that mistake again). But it is true that there are animal communication systems which might seem to provide the basis for human language: the trouble is that they do not. Animals survive well enough without a language of the kind that marks us out - and so do human beings. Even now that almost all adult humans speak, it is possible to survive, and breed, without that understanding: witness one language-impaired family identified by Gopnik. Whatever genetic change has caused this lack 'does not seem to impair overall intelligence; most of the afflicted family members score in the normal range of the non-verbal parts of IQ tests. (Indeed, Gopnik studied one unrelated child with the syndrome who routinely received the best grade in his mainstream math class.)' (Pinker p.49) Which may, of course, confirm what non-mathematicians have always suspected ...

Conversely, there are human beings who are fluent and irrepressible talkers who score very badly in IQ tests, and by ordinary standards of social and practical competence. 'Fluent grammatical language can appear in many kinds of people with severe intellectual impairments, like schizophrenics, Alzheimer's patients, some autistic children, and some aphasics' (Pinker p.52). Some of their talk is quite engaging. 'Ask a normal child to name some animals, and you will get the standard inventory of pet store and barnyard. Ask a Williams syndrome child, and you get a more interesting menagerie: unicorn, pteranodon, yak, ibex, water buffalo, sea lion, saber-tooth tiger, vulture, koala, dragon, and ... brontosaurus rex' (Pinker p.53) . It would be unkind to wonder whether the academic world contained large numbers of similarly disadvantaged speakers - but I shall be suggesting that the syndrome does reveal a truth about the academy, and about the point of language.

For the moment, it is enough to say that language is not directly explained by any evolutionary advantage of increased intelligence. 'Intelligence' is, in any case, a ragbag of assorted competencies, most of which most creatures manage well enough without. As one who lacks technical, mathematical, musical and athletic intelligences (at least), I am sure that merely verbal wit is not all we need. Adaptive behaviour, and even socially manipulative behaviour, does not need speech: witness squirrels, starlings, rats and chimpanzees. We cannot explain language, in an evolutionary setting, by referring to the present advantages of speech (such as they are): if language were to survive, and spread so successfully throughout our species gene-pool, it must have afforded a massive advantage from the very first beginning, and in its earliest, least developed form.

The obvious - but, it seems, irrelevant - response is as follows. Other animals - including birds and primates - use specific signals for items in their immediate environment. Vervet monkeys, for example, have distinct calls for different sorts of predator. Any social animal can signal different moods, and even identify distinct individuals. Once we have abandoned the absurd conviction that no other animals can think at all, it seems easy enough to think that human language is no more than a developed form of ordinary primate naming and expressive practice. We have evidence that primates (and other animals) can even make use of those naming and expressive practices for their own ends: chimpanzees can signal so as to deceive their peers. The signal, in short, is not an automatic response to an observed situation (not a 'natural' sign) but brought into play with a view to an imagined future. This is as if a bee, instead of dancing out the true directions to a flower patch, were to dance a phantom destination to divert the hive. Bees get no advantage from deception (and so do not deceive): chimpanzees, especially young chimpanzees, have need of tricks. Trickery depends on the trickster's recognition that others will respond predictably to certain signals: it requires, that is, a theory of mind, or (more concretely) an imagined other, moving in the trickster's own interior space. That in turn is possible because the animal has such an interior space, a sort of map which defines the spatial and social environment. As so often, we know that creatures have such maps by what they do when they do not have it: deprived of their maps they have to respond to single stimuli, and can no longer easily run mazes, or relocate hidden objects. A brain-damaged squid no longer follows fishes around corners, because (in effect) the fish has vanished in a way that would not affect a normal squid. A brain-damaged monkey cannot easily locate scattered grain (since every time it loses sight of a grain it has to relocate it from the start). Planned deception of the sort that chimpanzees routinely practice depends on their having more developed maps, ones that propose new, unseen destinations.

Primate (and other) intelligence is deceptive from the start, and though we do not need language to deceive, we can be confident that Kipling guessed correctly about its use. 'What was the first practical use Man made of [speech]? Remember he was, by that time, past-master in all arts of camouflage known to the beasts. ... In short he could *act* any kind of lie then extant. I submit, therefore, that the first use Man made of his new power of expression was to *tell* a lie - a frigid and calculated lie. Imagine the wonder and delight of the First Liar in the World when he found that the first lie overwhelmingly outdid every effort of his old mud-and-grass camouflages and with no expenditure of energy! Conceive his pride, his awestricken admiration of himself, when he saw that, by mere word of mouth, he could send his simpler companions shinning up trees in search of fruit that he knew was not there; and when they descended, empty and angry, he could persuade them that they, and not he, were in fault, and could dispatch them hopefully up another tree.' (Kipling p.233f: being part of his rectorial address at St.Andrews, in 1923)

But is manipulative intelligence the root of language? Once language exists, language-users can use it to gain advantages - precisely, over language-users. Those without language are immune to rhetoric, and may easily outperform their chattering peers. Energy and brain-space devoted to internalising vocabulary and linguistic rules is not available for other uses: is it obvious that the best singer is also the best hunter? The best liar will, no doubt, have great successes amongst those who listen - but the tribes who listened most attentively died off. And so it follows once again: if any ever spoke at all, then probably they died (glued, as it were, to soap opera) - and we cannot speak.

The Structure of Human Language

The animal systems, so it seems, do not help. Chomsky, who did so much to identify what is needed if anyone is to speak or understand a language, denies that human languages can be derived from animal communication systems (Hattiangadi p.178), precisely because our languages depend upon syntactic rules. On the one hand, Chomsky's theories fit well into an evolutionary framework. On the other hand, they constitute a problem. They fit well, because Chomsky'' refutation of behaviouristic analyses of language learning drew attention to the inherited behaviour patterns (call them, instincts) which psychologists had been neglecting. Whereas it had been fashionable to insist that all human talents were acquired by learning, it was then realised that even learning depends on unlearnt practices. Even the simple rule 'Repeat the movements that were reinforced last time' (on which behaviourist psychologists had sought to found all human culture) is one that cannot, logically, be 'learnt' at all: it is the (far too simple) rule for learning, and further requires some unlearnt rules of identifying what should count as 'the same movement'. What Chomsky further showed was that human infants do not learn languages just by repeating what they are praised for saying: the *rule* for forming plurals, or past tenses, or questions, is something that all normal children learn - but not because they have been taught it. They are primed to respond in accordance with appropriate rules to the signals (which only human infants readily perceive as signals) they receive. Gopnik's language-impaired family, asked to invent a plural form for the invented term *wug*, offers 'wugness', and for *zat*, tries 'zackle' (Pinker p.50). Later research has suggested that amongst the very early decision points in language-acquisition concerns word-order: in language-communities that follow Subject-Verb-Object order, there are prepositions; where the order is Subject-Object-Verb, there are postpositions (Pinker p.234). The order, Object-Subject-Verb, is apparently rare enough to make it suitable for alien-speak: it is the chosen form of the Jedi Master, Yoda (Crystal p.98). It is as if a child were choosing from an array of possible rules which, once accepted, clarify whole areas of language. Infants do not learn languages by rote: 'between the late-twos and the mid-threes, children's language blossoms into fluent grammatical conversation so rapidly that it overwhelms the researchers who study it, and no one has worked out the exact sequence' (Pinker p.269) - which is one reason why it is so difficult to see what 'half a grammar' might look like. It seems overwhelmingly likely that Universal Grammar is a species-specific feature of humanity, just like learning to walk. Infants learn to speak against almost all obstacles - as long as there is someone speaking round them. In this we are like song-birds, who also need to have been exposed to bird-song at a critical age, and who then pick out the species-specific songs to work with (for the analogy, see Aitchison pp.7ff). They, like us, develop dialects.

Where Chomsky's theories do not fit so easily into an evolutionary frame (as he says himself) is just that there is no precedent for Universal Grammar, that it is a single, shattering mutation. Non-linguistic systems of communication allow only a finite number of discrete communications: human languages permit an infinite number. It will always be possible to create a sentence no-one ever used before, and know that it will be understood by any speaker of the relevant language. The power of language is infinitely in excess of anything that a practical animal would need: even if our present linguistic capacity arrived (as seems quite likely) by degrees, that transformation from the finite to the infinite was not a matter of degree. But such rapid shifts are not ones that evolutionary theorists can accommodate: the point of neo-Darwinian theory (even in the mouths of 'punctuated equilibrists') is that change from one generation to the next is gradual, that there are no really novel organs or behaviour patterns despite the differences eventually made. Nor is it plausible to require that literally every human being has Universal Grammar: neo-Darwinian theory eschews essentialism (see Hattiangadi). Humankind is not a natural kind in the sense that once we imagined (see my paper on the question whether Humanity is a Natural Kind). There may be many of our conspecifics who lack whatever trait it is that we identify as 'most important' - and indeed there are, as has already been observed, human beings who are variously aphasic. The unity of humankind, and the necessity of equal respect for all that is human, are moral and not biological theses, which do not depend upon the truth of Chomsky's rationalist revolution - though it is encouraging to realise that even if we were all compelled to learn an Orwellian Newspeak our children would create a new language out of it, and say exactly what they pleased, resistant to the postulated tyranny of language. The theory remains convincing, but if we are to avoid postulating an unprecedented alteration somewhere in our lineage, we still need to find the evolutionary roots of Universal Grammar. It is not enough to reply, with Pinker (pp.342, 362ff), that it is no more surprising that human speech is uniquely human than that only elephants have trunks: we can guess what elephants' trunks evolved from, by imperceptible degrees, while still remaining doubtful about Universal Grammar.

What does that Grammar consist in? It is apparently universally true that sentences (a term for which there is no wholly satisfactory definition, but which seems to identify meaningful sequences of signs) are compounded from noun-phrases and verb-phrases. The transformations of indicative sentences into interrogative or imperative ones, or of positive into negative ones, demand a recognition of those divisions into phrases. Even children do not make mistakes about deep structures (unless of course the sentences are genuinely ambiguous: Pinker p.102 cites, amongst others, 'we sell gasoline to anyone in a glass container'). It is the power to handle transformations which identifies true language, and that power seems to be instinctual, not learnt. Whether apes can display a corresponding ability is moot: some contend that no ape has done more than string terms together, without any grasp of grammar. So far, at least, there is no widespread acceptance of Ape Language: there seem to be no clear examples of transformations, nor of other syntactic features seemingly typical of human speech, such as recursiveness or embeddedness. On the evidence so far, the other primates diverged from our own ancestral line before the change or changes that produced Universal Grammar. If this is so, we still do not have our missing links, and must use our imaginations on the fossils of *australopithecus afarensis*, *homo habilis*, *erectus* or *sapiens neanderthalensis*. Neanderthals have suffered most from changing ideological fashions: sometimes they are 'dumb savages', incapable of human speech because their throats are too much like apes; sometimes their throats are more like ours, and they can manage to string terms together, but not syntactically; sometimes they speak very much like us, and lost the evolutionary race by accident. In the absence of clear evidence, they serve as images of what might have been (but almost certainly was not).

One route to understanding, a little estranged from Chomsky, may be to place unusual emphasis on what we *write*. Pinker observes that speech may be an instinct, but not writing (p.189), but it can be argued that the written form is older. If human language enables us to consider absent or wholly non-existent entities, so also do animal markers. By laying scents around a territory an animal ensures its 'presence' to intruders. Those may be 'natural' signs, but it is not so difficult to imagine their transformation into 'given' signs: ones that only affect a given local group, or can be used to deceive. Whatever change it was that brought about humanity enabled our ancestors to make iconic marks: signs which signify in virtue of their perceived similarity to the things signified (symbolic marks, by contrast, do not resemble what they mean). Our ancestors seem - if the cave paintings can be trusted - to have acted out the parts of other creatures, and to have portrayed them. The picture theory of meaning, though long discredited as an account of speech, may be literally true of pictures. Chinese ideograms, Egyptian hieroglyphs and Sumerian cuneiform alike take their beginning from iconic marks - admittedly a long time after we presume that speech began (but did it?). European theories, ever since Aristotle, have treated writing as representing speech, and speech as representing thoughts. It has been fashionable of late to deny that there could be wordless thoughts to represent. That particular thesis flies in the face of anecdote, experiment and evolutionary likelihood. But it may be worth rejecting the other half of European commonsense, that speech comes earlier than writing. Such ideograms need not have grammar: in that sense, they offer no solution to the major problem, but rather make it clearer still that we did not *need* grammar to communicate. ‘Writing’ creates living presences that I have called ‘icons’.

Picture language, I should make clear, is not mere replication: it is not as if we always first identified ‘the real thing’ and only then portrayed it on convenient surfaces. The portrayal begins with the identification, the drawing of a line - in imagined space and time - around the chosen entity. Most of those lines, no doubt, are drawn for us: not that all rational creatures everywhere must ‘obviously’ divide the world up in the way we do (remember *gavagai*), but simply that we do. Folk biology across the world agrees that there are obvious *kinds* of living creature, and that such creatures are *the same* from birth to death (Pinker pp.421ff). Children do not wonder whether some novel term ('a dax') could mean 'a dog or its bone' (Pinker p.156) or 'a dog's ear and my finger'. 'Gavagai', after all, almost certainly means 'rabbi'', not rabbit-meat or rabbit-slice or rapidly-moving brownness. Icons can also be placed in an implicit order: rabbits are sorts of furry creatures, which are sorts of animals. Children across the world insist that animals and artefacts are different sorts of thing: a coffee-pot can be turned into a bird-feeder, but not a racoon into a skunk (Pinker p.424). What is not entirely natural, perhaps, is the way we map these divisions onto other things: our instinct dictates that rabbits are countable, living creatures, but not that rocks or areas of sand are entities. We make them entities by fixing our memories upon them, whether subjectively or by agreement.

Once, on a glittering ice-field, ages and ages ago,
Ung, a maker of pictures, fashioned an image of snow.
Fashioned the form of a tribesman - gaily he whistled and sung,
Working the snow with his fingers. *Read ye the story of Ung!* (Kipling p.342)

Kipling's neolithic artist learnt to be pleased that his fellow tribesmen could not see so clearly, even though this sometimes made them doubt his images. But maybe, in prehistorical fact, the story was rather different: each member of the tribe made its own adjustments to the snowman till all were agreed in finding the man 'there' (though only 'in a way'). Of course, if their individual adjustments cancelled each other out, and they were left at last with only a grubby heap of snow, they probably were not a tribe much longer. Those who managed to co-operate in releasing their individual visions from the snow were united. I say, deliberately, 'releasing': the original visualisers fixed their icon in a heap of snow, or a rock, and let it out of its imprisoning surrounds. Flint hand-axes are not carved out at random, but seen within the flint: what is not part of the vision is then flaked away.

Those portraits were available to any single moment - but any larger portrayal (larger than could be seen at a moment) required us to hold them in memory as we travelled round. Maybe there are other ways of bringing things to mind than literal travel across a memory-laden landscape. Wills cites Bruce Chatwin's Songlines on the subject of aboriginal songs:

Regardless of the words, it seems the melodic contour of the song describes the nature of the land over which the song passes. So, if the Lizard Man were dragging his heels across the salt pans of Lake Eyre, you could expect a succession of long flats, like Chopin's "Funeral March". If he were skipping up and down the MacDonnell escarpments, you would have a series of arpeggios and glissandos, like Liszt's Hungarian rhapsodies (Chatwin, cited by Wills p.147).

These techniques bring past and future and imagined possibility together. We act them out in portraiture and music, and can conceive how tribes together might begin to sing the same song, model the same snowman. Language, on this account, begins in metaphor, in acting out an assembly of memories and hopes through landscaping and song. Prehistorical accident dictates the precise 'conventions' used to invoke the memories. Those conventions need not have been explicitly agreed (since they could not have been): but they could be tacitly agreed, as oarsmen adjust their motions to their partners' - or else drown. Before there was syntactical language, language 'properly so-called', there were the mansions of the house of memory - and some of those houses could represent 'future' states of the world, ones reached (in lived experience) by waiting. Which is how, despite Wittgensteinian[3] dogma, a non-language user could 'expect its master to be back tomorrow': the icon of its master is in a distant imagined place, which is growing closer by the minute.

But still we have no syntax. Where that might arise is from the fact that public icons (snowmen or carved sticks) are items in the public world which might in their turn be represented by an icon. An icon might represent Ung's snowman, and not just the man that the snowman itself stood for. Maybe - with much more difficulty - there might even be an icon cancelling Ung's snowman. There are still no signs (necessarily symbolic signs) to make clear the role of different icons in a complex whole: no signs for 'the' or 'of' or 'if' (whose marks can hardly be iconic). That just happened.

Was the arrival of syntax an unmixed blessing? On the contrary, it could be said, ideograms or musics represent events in ways (some hold) superior to the noun-verb structures we locate in language. Maybe even they have faults: reality is seamless, it is said. Essences exist by virtue only of the language in which they are expressed, and a 'truer' portrayal of the world is as ever-shifting fire, uncountable and unrepeated. Folk taxonomies exist, to be sure, but maybe that is an artistic fashion, something imposed once we had invented language as a system of

---

[3] Wittgenstein, Ludwig (1889-1951), Viennese-born philosopher who worked in Cambridge and was concerned with the scope and limits of language. Reference entry in A Dictionary of Philosophy, Ed. Speake J. Publisher Pan Books Ltd., 1979. (Editor's Note)

discrete signifiers, signifying 'things' that did not exist until we spoke of them. The iconic signs were works of art (and so in a way misleading), but at least they represented or created wholes. When (and why) did we come to think of the world as made up of things, on the one hand, and their changing qualities and relations on the other? 'The units of animal communication convey whole chunks of information (rough equivalents of *I am angry, You may may mate with me, A predator just* appeared). Language breaks up those chunks in a way that, to the best of our knowledge, no animal communication system has ever done' (Bickerton p.11). Augustine at one time suspected that language was a function of the Fall, a source of division and unclarity (Rist p.38)

Robert Graves poses the problem:

"Children are dumb to say how hot the day is,
How hot the scent is of the summer rose,
How dreadful the black wastes of evening sky,
How dreadful the tall soldiers drumming by.

But we have speech to chill the angry day,
And speech, to dull the rose's cruel scent.
We spell away the overhanging night,
We spell away the soldiers and the fright.

There's a cool web of language winds us in,
Retreat from too much joy or too much fear:
We grow sea-green at last and coldly die
In brininess and volubility,

But if we let our tongues lose self-possession,
Throwing off language and its watery clasp
Before our death, instead of when death comes,
Facing the wide glare of the children's day,
Facing the rose, the dark sky and the drums,
We shall go mad no doubt and die that way."
(Graves p.37)

Some have doubted that human languages were universally dependent on that subject-predicate dichotomy, but their case is weak. Strangely, they are often the same people as claim that there is no thought without language of one sort or another, that our form of speech determines how we think - so that wordless appreciation of reality is at once impossible and the only truthful stance. Whorf's claims about Hopi (that Hopi-speakers were better attuned to a post-Einsteinian world than English-speakers) seem to rest mostly upon bad translations. 'No one is really sure how Whorf came up with his outlandish claims, but his limited, badly analysed sample of Hopi speech and his long-time leanings towards mysticism must have contributed' (Pinker p.63). Bloom's corresponding argument, that Mandarin Chinese is *less* appropriate for a shifty world than English, since it cannot handle counterfactuals, is founded on better evidence, but can also be rebutted (Pinker pp.66f). In the absence of good counterexamples, it seems reasonable to reaffirm that human languages depend on our identifying substances, and being capable of imagining what is not there. And maybe those two features, put together, do give a further clue to syntax - without quite accepting the pessimistic conclusion that language divides us from a true appreciation of the real.

The One Original Language

Psamtik's experiment was bound to fail. But something like it has been observed. Derek Bickerton has proposed that infants reared by pidgin speakers make their own creoles. Pidgins are hardly languages at all: speakers are compelled to use mere collocations of a small set of terms to convey their meanings to people with whom they share no language. Pidgins, in fact, are slightly more complex, more useful versions of the sort of speech which the aphasic or feral children or (maybe) Washoe perpetrate. But children, reared in this climate, make up grammars (Bickerton pp. 121f, 169ff). One spectacular recent example (featured on BBC2's Horizon on 3 April 1997) is the development of Idioma de Signos Nicaraguense from Lenguaje de Signos Nicaraguense (Pinker p.36f). The latter, LSN, is a pidgin used by deaf children who had been reared in ordinary households without any chance to learn an official sign-language. They had had to communicate entirely by mime, and when they were introduced to each other those different mimes formed the basis of a pidgin: 'everyone uses it differently, and the signers depend on suggestive, elaborate circumlocutions rather than on a consistent grammar'. But younger deaf children in Nicaragua's schools have created a full creole, in which subjects, verbs and objects, as well as the mood, tense and structure of the sentences, are clear. Bickerton further suggests that the grammar of creole languages is more like that of other creoles than that of the parent languages that fed the pidgin (Pinker p.35f)[4]. If this

[4] An alternative explanation, that many creoles have some historical connection with a Portuguese pidgin called Sabir (Crystal p.337), does not explain the similarities of creoles with no such European background.

turns out to be true, we have a window into the preferred workings of the language instinct (though not, of course, the only possible, or the best, workings).

On this account our hominid ancestors created something like a pidgin, in which they could draw their own and others' attention to particular aspects of the world (the 'real' world and the world of hope and memory). Public images (like Ung's snowman or like communcal dance-music) gave that pidgin a larger range than any animal communication system. At some point in our history - maybe on the emergence of *Homo sapiens sapiens* - children were born who made a sort of creole out of the pidgin that they heard. We are no closer to conceiving what the relevant mutation might have been, but slightly closer to seeing how it might have worked. We do not need to conceive that 'dumb and beastly savages' invented language, but rather that there were hominids speaking or singing or gesturing or modelling in 'protolanguage', and that children reared in that environment might do what they have done since then: namely, disentangle nouns and verbs, and create a grammar.

And why was it useful? For the very same reason as it has been useful since for children to have a secret language, unknown to their elders - or their rival gangs. In a highly mobile society we have almost forgotten how much life-chances rest on the esteem and the co-operation of our age-cohorts. Back in the palaeolithic era the first linguists had a supremely secret tongue, a grand conspiracy against their elders and an opportunity to identify the routes from *here* to an imagined *there*. Their elders could already speak of non-existent or of distant things: without a clear grammar they could not trace the differences between what was here and what was not, nor notice what *might* have happened if.... Nor could they easily transform indicative utterances into questions or commands: rather, there was no difference in protolanguage between the imperative and indicative moods. Nor, until there was language, could we grasp that some of our iconic signs were simply false (though they could be deceitful). As Plato showed (in The Sophist), we need to distinguish subjects and what is said of them if we are to handle falsehood. We need to grasp not only 'being-as-such' but also 'being such and such', not only the existential but the predicative 'is'. But that is by the way.

In those days it was not *children* who were dumb, but adults. Our children probably believe this is still true.

One of the triumphs of nineteenth-century philology was the plausible reconstruction of Indo-European (and an associated romantic reconstruction of the way of life that the first Indo-European speakers lived). Since then philologists have postulated Norstratic (from which grew Indo-European, Afro-Asiatic, Dravidian, Altaic, Uralic and Eskimo-Aleut), Sino-Caucasian-Amerind-Nostratic, 'covering Eurasia and the Americas', and at long last 'Proto-World', spoken perhaps by mitochondrial Eve but just as probably not, between sixty thousand and a million years ago (see Pinker pp.256f; Wills pp.22-57). The chances are that the change from protolanguage to language occurred just once, in some briefly favoured environment where chatter did not distract our ancestors from other dangers. Our chances of reconstructing that original are small: none of the same words need have survived this long, nor any particular grammatic structure. Common forms, by this time, are more probably coincidences or horizontal borrowings, not inherited vocabulary. Romantic reconstructions of the Way We Lived are just as likely to be beside the point. No present-day societies, not even hunter-gatherers, are 'undeveloped', any more than any present languages are 'primitive'. Some South American Indians are hunter-gatherers because their recent ancestors preferred the forest to the cities. Biological evolution is not orthogenetic: how much less linguistic? Anglophones too easily believe that English is 'more evolved' as lacking genders or inflections: in fact there is good reason to suspect that English has ten genders (judging from the different pronouns reckoned appropriate to different sorts of thing), and has fewer inflections only because its grammatical indicators are conventionally separated from main words. Nor is there any general reason to think that the more differentiated languages are either earlier or later than the less.

Nor is there any good reason to suppose, as many commentators do, that we were once more 'literal' than now. Why should we suppose that those first speaking children (or their protolinguistic parents) talked first of things that we would reckon 'physical'? If the picture I have sketched, of memory-laden maps, is accurate our ancestors confronted a world in which ghostly associations and projected hopes were obvious. It was once 'literally' true that gods and animals spoke to us, in ways that we would now consider hallucinatory. It took millenia to convince a few of us that 'physical realities' were paramount: until that conviction dawned we had no reason to learn our language only from the 'physical' (see Barfield). Children - and adults - play, and the object of their exercise is not, as Augustine reckoned, truth. 'Therefore,' so he said (Encheiridion 22.7), 'to use words for deceit, not for the purpose for which they were instituted, is a sin' (see Kirwan p.198). But this is even more erroneous than thinking that the purpose of sex is procreation: remember Kipling's Liar.

Augustine himself gives a reason against the associated axiom that the purpose of language is transparent association. It seems to be the nature of language that it diversifies: we are always inventing - especially the young are always inventing - dialects. And this is by the providence of God. 'The diversity of tongues divides human beings from each other. ... Thanks to that diversity of tongues alone, their similar natures have so little power to make them friends, that someone may enjoy the company of his dog more than of a foreigner' (City of God 19.7). Each generation modifies its mother tongue to make its secret dialect, its own badge of belonging. Speed or clarity of communication across the generations or the nations is of little weight: what matters is our wish to build a world, and make sure that only those with the proper passwords can have access to it.

'The amount of Truth open to Mankind has always been limited. Substantially, it comes to no more than the axiom ....: "That that is, is". Conversely, "That that is not, is not". But it is just this Truth that Man most bitterly resents being brought to his notice. He will do, suffer, and permit anything rather than acknowledge it. He desires that the waters which he has dug and canalised should run up hill by themselves when it suits him. He desires that the numerals which he has himself counted on his fingers and christened "two and two" should make three and five according to his varying needs and moods. Why does he want this? Because subconsciously, he still scales himself against his age-old companions, the beasts, who can only act lies.' (Kipling 1928, pp.234ff).

Even the thought that we might wish for clarity or accuracy between ourselves may go too far. Perhaps it is true that the gift of language has given its best performers social advantages: 'anthropologists have noted that tribal chiefs are often both gifted orators and highly polygynous'

(Pinker p.369) - but whoever said or thought that *rhetoric* aimed at the truth, or even at clarification? Sperber suggests that talk was originally peacocking, a way of pulling mates: work was made bearable by assimilation to courtship (Lecercle p.143). Long before courtship, children chatter their way to fortune (Hattiangadi pp.191ff). Who supposes that they care about 'the truth'? 'The poetic imagination constructs a cosmos of its own' (Frye p.xxii: Danesi p.81). Children construct the games that some of their number win: the dream of external judgement is late coming. We do not much want that 'real truth', and would not necessarily gain by it. Do you *want* to know the whole truth about yourself? *Should* you want to know the whole truth about another?

My suggestion is close to Dunbar's, but not quite the same. His thesis is that our enlarged vocabularies, and our recursive grammars, are needed if we are to cope with large assemblies of our conspecifics. Most human conversation, on his account, is not to do with where the antelopes have hidden, or where the best field mushrooms can be found, but rather with personal relationships. We need to imagine not just what one other person will do, but what that one imagines that another two or three will do or try to do. We need to chat about it as our substitute for grooming.

"Lou is telling Anne what Molly
Said to Mark behind her back;
Jack likes Jill who worships George
Who has the hots for Jack ...

Willy cannot bear his father,
Lilian is afraid of kids;
The Love that rules the sun and stars
Permits what He forbids.

Adrian's pleasure-loving dachsund
In a sinner's lap lies curled;
Drunken absent-minded fingers
Pat a sinless world.

Who is Jenny lying to
In her call, Collect, to Rome?
The Love that made her out of nothing
Tells me to go home."
(Auden p.310)

No doubt Dunbar is right in his account of what we mostly do (and have done from the beginning). Whether he is right to suppose that we have needed this enlarged vocabulary, this more complex theory of mind, to identify the many more relationships involved in larger groupings than the other primates, and that we have needed those larger groups in order to cope with scavenging in the savanna, remains more doubtful: one more speculative fiction that might perhaps be fact. On my account the unexpectable arrival of children with the gift of grammar perhaps took place within a smaller group, and 'accidentally' allowed the creation of a larger, diverting fiction from its proper task.

"But should we want to gossip all the time,
Were fact not fiction for us at its best,
Or find a charm in syllables that rhyme,
Were not our fate by verbal chance expressed,
As rustics in a ring-dance pantomime
The Knight at some lone cross-roads of his quest?"
(Auden p.321)

Whereas really 'dumb animals' are bound to see clearly all that is of interest to them (unless it is hidden), beasts on the point of speaking are confronted by life-worlds containing memories and phantoms of what might yet be, as well as visions of what others see. It is at least imaginable that some sorts of pidgin or protolanguage might be available to them: 'literal' only in the sense that it reports the obviously true. True language arises in a favoured environment, where those who can create a grammar have an opportunity to disentangle and categorise aspects of different ideograms. Because we can safely see both more and less than what is 'there' we can make non-biological choices. The point is not only, as Bickerton suggests (pp.250ff), that social representations are non-negotiable, so that we may prefer to die, in biological reality, rather than lose our (imvented) selves. Our childish ancestors, by creating shared realms of fantasy that later enabled them to work together, also left it open that there was a 'real world' distinct from the species-significant 'obvious'. 'The Truth', Democritus told us, 'loves to hide' (although the Greek for Truth is heard as 'What is Not Hidden'). One example of that Hidden Truth is the Otherworld (in Greek, the Unseen), the realm where we may hope to co-create, at least if we are heroes. Another is the World as modern science defines it, far removed from the species-significant world of (sometime) common sense. The very notion of a 'real Truth', against whose standard most of our more ordinary perceptions are delusions, is an artefact. I do not mean - as some postmodern writers think they mean - that Truth itself is an artefact: that there is a Truth, compounded of the presences identified in accurate, iconic representation, and that those presences are what the One, the Good, or God, requires are axioms. What is puzzling (and is a forgotten argument for theism) is that we have access to that Truth[5]

---

[5] I have argued this point at length, for example in <u>God's World and the Great Awakening</u> (Clarendon Press:

"In that ago when being was believing,
Truth was the most of many credibles,
More first, more always than a bat-winged lion,
A fish-tailed dog or eagle-headed fish,
The least like mortals, doubted by their deaths.

Truth was their model as they strove to build
A world of lasting objects to believe in,
Without believing earthernware and legend,
Archway and song, were truthful or untruthful:
The Truth was there already to be true."
(Auden p.306)

As long as we were only aware of our own world, wordlessly present to us, we had no way of making any distinction between our world and the Truth. Even when we could speak, syntactically, and incorporate a sense of others' points of view, we were still hampered. If there had only been one language we would too easily have equated our own story with the real world's, with God's: the tower we sought to raise to heaven was perhaps no 'real' building, but the single tongue itself. The fate of the monolingual is to find things 'obvious' that are not, and to be prevented from transcending their own tongue by the lack of any other convenient vehicle. It is a fate that seems to be befalling recent scientists, who think that nothing which is excluded from 'scientific language' can be real. Hard experience may teach them that there are other tongues. 'I have no doubt that this is all divinely predetermined, so that pride may be subdued by hard work and intellects which tend to despise things that are easily discovered may be rescued from boredom and reinvigorated' (Augustine DDC 2.10: Green

---

Oxford 1991).

p.61; see Rist p 36). Somehow, we must suppose, the languages we speak *can* carve the world at its own joints (as Plato hoped: Phaedrus 265) - but more often carve *our* world. The Truth that was there already, and the many Fictions that language and protolanguage let us make, have both their parts to play in human life and learning. That, after all, is the miracle.

Aitchison, Jean (1996) The Seeds of Speech: Language Origin and Evolution (Cambridge University Press: Cambridge)

Auden, W.H. (1966) Collected Shorter Poems 1927-57 (Faber: London)

Augustine (1995) De Doctrina Christiana, ed. R.P.H.Green (Clarendon Press: Oxford)

Barfield, Owen (1952) Poetic Diction (Faber: London; 1st edition 1928)

Bickerton, Derek (1990) Language and Species (University of Chicago Press: Chicago)

Bloom, A.H. (1981) The Linguistic Shaping of Thought: a study of the impact of language on thinking in China and the West (Erlbaum: Hillsdale, New Jersey)

Cooper, A. (1987) 'Chinese Evidence on Language': Richard L.Gregory, ed., The Oxford Companion to the Mind (Oxford University Press: Oxford), pp.142-6

Crystal, David (1987) The Cambridge Encyclopedia of Language (Cambridge University Press: Cambridge)

Danesi, Marcel (1993) Vico, Metaphor and the Origin of Language (Indiana University Press: Bloomington & Indianapolis)

Dunbar, Robin (1996) Grooming, Gossip and the Evolution of Language (Faber: London)

Frye, Northrop (1990) Words with Power (Penguin: Harmondsworth)

Glidden, David K. (1994) `Parrots, Pyrrhonists and Native Speakers': Stephen Everson, ed., Language (Cambridge University Press: Cambridge) pp.129-48.

Graves, Robert (1975) Collected Poems (Cassell: London)

Hattiangadi, J.N. (1987) How is Language Possible? Philosophical Reflections on the Evolution of Language and Knowledge (Open Court: La Salle, Illinois)

Kenny, A.J.P. (1973) `The Origin of Language': A.J.P.Kenny, H.C.Longuet-Higgins, J.R.Lucas & C.H.Waddington The Development of Mind (Edinburgh University Press: Edinburgh), pp.91-100

Kipling, Rudyard (1927) Verse: 1885-1926 (Hodder & Stoughton: London)

Kipling, Rudyard (1928) A Book of Words: selections from speeches and addresses delivered between 1906 and 1927 (Macmillan: London)

Kirwan, Christopher (1994) 'Augustine on the Nature of Speech': Stephen Everson, ed., Language (Cambridge University Press: Cambridge) pp.188-211

Lecercle, Jean-Jacques (1985) Philosophy through the Looking-Glass (Hutchinson & Co: London)

Long, A.A. & Sedley, D.N. (1987) edds, The Hellenistic Philosophers (Cambridge University Press: Cambridge)

Muir, Edwin (1960) Collected Poems 1921-58 (Faber: London)

Pinker, Steven (1994) The Language Instinct: the new science of language and the mind (Allen Lane: London)

Rist, J.M. (1994) Augustine (Cambridge University Press: Cambridge)

Wills, Christopher (1993) The Runaway Brain: the evolution of human uniqueness (Harper Collins: London)

THE SECOND GOWLAND LECTURE
(THE ELEVENTH ANNUAL LECTURE OF THE INITIATIVE)

EVOLUTION AND THEOLOGY TODAY

REV. DR. ARTHUR R. PEACOCKE

Formerly Director of the Ramsey Centre, St. Cross College

"Darwinism appeared, and, under the disguise of a foe, did the work of a friend. It has conferred upon philosophy and religion an inestimable benefit, by shewing us that we must choose between two alternatives. Either God is everywhere present in nature, or He is nowhere."

(Aubrey Moore, in the 12th edition of *Lux Mundi,* 1891, p.73).

1. Introduction

It would, no doubt, come as a surprise to many of the biologically-cultured 'despisers of the Christian religion', to learn that, as increasingly thorough historical investigations are showing[1], the nineteenth-century reaction to Darwin in theological and ecclesiastical circles was much more positive and welcoming than the legends propagated by both popular and academic biological publications are prepared to admit.

---

[1] E.g., J.R. Moore, *The Post-Darwinian Controversies: a study of the Protestant struggle to come to terms with Darwin in Great Britain and America* (Cambridge: Cambridge University Press, 1979); J.R. Lucas, "Wilberforce and Huxley: a legendary encounter", *The Historical Journal* 22,2 (1979):313-330; J.V. Jensen, "Return to the Huxley-Wilberforce Debate", *Brit.J.Hist.Sci. 21 (1988):161-179.*

Furthermore, the scientific reaction was also much more negative than usually depicted, those sceptical of Darwin's ideas including initially *inter alia* the leading comparative anatomist of his day, Richard Owen (a Cuverian[2]), and the leading geologist, Charles Lyell. Many theologians deferred judgement, but the proponents of at least one strand in theology in nineteenth-century England chose to intertwine their insights closely with the Darwinian - that 'catholic' revival in the Church of England of a stress on the doctrine of the Incarnation and its extension into the sacraments and so of a renewed sense of the sacramentality of nature and God's immanence in the world. More of the nineteenth-century theological reaction to Darwin was constructive and reconciling in temper than practically any biological authors today will allow.

That is perhaps not surprising in view of the background to at least T.H. Huxley's aggressive propagation of Darwin's ideas and his attacks on Christianity, namely that of the clerical restriction of opportunities for biological scientists in England in the nineteenth century. His principal agenda was the establishment of science as a profession independent of ecclesiastical control - and in this we can sympathise. So it is entirely understandable that the present, twentieth-century *zeitgeist* of the world of biological science is that of viewing 'religion' as the opposition, if no longer in any way a threat. This tone saturates the writings of the biologists Richard Dawkins and Stephen Gould and many others - and even philosophers such as Daniel Dennett.

---

[2] Follower of Baron Georges Cuvier, (1769-1832) who interpreted the fossil remains of animals by relating them to the Genesis account of the flood and rejected theories of evolution. His classification system of animals was widely accepted in pre-Darwinian biology. (Editors Note)

This has polarised the scene, but what I do find even more surprising, and less understandable, is the way in which the 'disguised friend' of Darwinism, more generally of evolutionary ideas, has been admitted (if at all) only grudgingly, with many askance and sidelong looks, into the parlours of Christian theology. (It was only last year that the Pope finally admitted that evolution was an established fact!) I believe it is vital for this churlishness to be rectified in this last decade of the twentieth century if the Christian religion (indeed any religion) is to be believable and have intellectual integrity enough to command even the attention, let alone the assent, of thoughtful people in the beginning of the next millennium.

2. Biological Evolution and God's Relation to the Living World

Let us first consider various features and characteristics of biological evolution and any theological reflections to which they may give rise.

2.1 Continuity and Emergence

A notable aspect of the scientific account of the natural world in general is the seamless character of the web that has been spun on the loom of time: the process appears as continuous from its cosmic 'beginning', in the 'hot big bang', to the present and at no point do modern natural scientists have to invoke any non-natural causes to explain their observations and inferences about the past.

The processes that have occurred can be characterised as *emergence*, for new forms of matter, and a hierarchy of organisation of these forms themselves, appear in the course of time. To these new organisations of matter it is, very often, possible to ascribe new levels of what can only be called 'reality': In other words new kinds of reality may be said to 'emerge' in time. Notably, on the surface of the Earth, new forms of *living* matter (that is, living organisms) have come into existence by this continuous process - that is what we mean by evolution.

What the scientific perspective of the world, especially the living world, inexorably impresses upon us is a *dynamic* picture of the world of entities and structures involved in continuous and incessant change and in process without ceasing. The scientific perspective of a cosmos, and in particular that of the biological world, as in development all the time must re-introduce into our understanding of God's creative relation to the world a dynamic element which was always implicit in the Hebrew conception of a 'living God', dynamic in action - even if obscured by the tendency to think of 'creation' as an event in the past. Any notion of God as Creator must now take into account, that God is continuously creating, continuously giving existence to, what is new; that God is *semper Creator*; that the world is a *creatio continua*. The traditional notion of God *sustaining* the world in its general order and structure now has to be enriched by a dynamic and creative dimension - the model of God sustaining and giving continuous existence to a process which has an inbuilt creativity, built into it by God. God is creating at every moment of the world's existence in and through the perpetually-endowed creativity of the very stuff of the world. God indeed makes 'things make themselves', as Charles Kingsley put it in *The Water Babies*.

Thus it is that the scientific perspective, and especially that of biological evolution, impels us to take more seriously and more concretely than hitherto the notion of the immanence of God-as-Creator - that God is the Immanent Creator *creating in and through the processes of the natural order*. I would urge that all this has to be taken in a very strong sense. If one asks where do we see God-as-Creator during, say, the processes of biological evolution, one has to reply: "The processes themselves, as unveiled by the biological sciences, *are* God-acting-as-Creator, God *qua* Creator." (This is not pantheism for it is the *action* of God that is identified with the creative processes of nature, not God's own self.) The processes are not themselves God, but the *action* of God-as-Creator. God gives existence in divenely-created time to a process that itself brings forth the new: thereby God is creat*ing*. This means we do not have to look for any extra supposed gaps in which, or mechanisms whereby, God might be supposed to be acting as Creator in the living world.

The model of musical composition for God's activity in creation is here, I would suggest, particularly helpful. There is no doubt of the 'transcendence' of the composer in relation to the music he or she creates - the composer gives it existence and without the composer it would not be at all. So the model properly reflects, as do all those of artistic creativity, that transcendence of God as Creator of all-that-is which, as 'listeners' to the music of creation, we wish to aver. For when we are actually listening to a musical work, say, a Beethoven piano sonata, then there are times when we are so deeply absorbed in it that, for a moment we are thinking Beethoven's musical thoughts with him. In such moments the

'music is heard so deeply
That it is not heard at all, but you are the music
While the music lasts'[3]

Yet if anyone were to ask at that moment, "*Where* is Beethoven now?" - we could only reply that Beethoven-*qua*-composer was to be found only in the music

[3] T.S. Eliot, 'The Dry Salvages', *The Four Quartets,* 11.

210-12.

itself. The music would in some sense be Beethoven's inner musical thought kindled in us and we would genuinely be encountering Beethoven-*qua*-composer. This very closely models, I am suggesting, God's immanence in creation and God's self-communication in and through the processes by means of which God is creating. The processes revealed by the sciences, especially evolutionary biology, are in themselves God-acting-as-Creator. There is no need to look for God as some kind of *additional* factor supplementing the processes of the world. God, to use language usually applied in sacramental theology, is 'in, with and under' all-that-is and all-that-goes-on.

2.2 The Mechanism of Biological Evolution

There appear to be no serious biologists who doubt that natural selection is a factor operative in biological evolution—and most would say it is by far the most significant one. At one end of the spectrum authors like Richard Dawkins argue cogently for the all-sufficiency of natural selection in explaining the course of biological evolution. However, other biologists are convinced that, even when the subtleties of natural selection are taken into account, it is not the whole story and some even go so far as to say that natural selection alone cannot account for speciation, the formation of distinctly new species. Some other considerations which, it is claimed, are needed to be taken into account are said to be: the 'evolution of evolvability', the constraints and selectivity effected by self-organisational principles; how an organism might evolve is a consequence of itself, 'genetic assimilation'; the innovative behaviour of an individual living creature in a particular environment; 'top-down causation' (or 'whole-part constraint') in evolution through a flow of information; much molecular evolutionary change is immune to natural selection, *group* selection (after all!); long-term changes resulting from 'molecular drive' (gene-hopping); effects of the context of adaptive change and *stasis.*

What is significant about all these proposals is that they are all operating entirely within a naturalistic framework and assume a basically Darwinian process to be operating, even when they disagree about its speed and smoothness. That being so, it has to be recognised that the history of life on earth involves chance in a way unthinkable before Darwin. there is a creative interplay of 'chance' and law apparent in the evolution of living matter by natural selection.

The original mutational events are random with respect to the future of the biological organism, even its future survival, but these changes have their consequences in a milieu that has regular and lawlike features. For the biological niche in which the organism exists then filters out, by the processes of natural selection, those changes in the DNA that enable the organisms possessing them to produce more progeny.

The interplay between 'chance', at the molecular level of the DNA, and 'law' or 'necessity' at the statistical level of the population of organisms tempted Jacques Monod, in *Chance and Necessity*[4] to elevate 'chance' to the level almost of a metaphysical principle whereby the universe might be interpreted. As is well known, he concluded that the 'stupendous edifice of evolution' is, in this sense, rooted in 'pure chance' and that *therefore* all inferences of direction or purpose in the development of the biological world, in particular, and of the universe, in general, must be false.

---

[4] Jacques Monod, *Chance and Necessity* (London: Collins, 1972).

The responses to this theses and attack on theism - mainly, it is interesting to note, from theologically informed scientists, and some philosophers, rather than from theologians - have been well surveyed by D.J. Bartholomew[5] and their relative strengths and weaknesses analysed. I shall here pursue what I consider to be the most fruitful line of theological reflection on the processes that Monod so effectively brought to the attention of the twentieth century - a direction that I began[6] to pursue in response to Monod and which has been further developed by the statistically-informed treatment of Bartholomew.

There is no reason why the randomness of molecular event in relation to biological consequence has to be given the significant metaphysical status that Monod attributed to it. The involvement of what we call 'chance' at the level of mutation in the DNA does not, of itself, preclude these events from displaying regular trends and manifesting inbuilt propensities at the higher levels of organisms, populations and eco-systems. To call the mutation of the DNA a 'chance' event serves simply to stress its randomness with respect to biological consequence. As I have earlier put it (in a response later supported and amplified by others):

> 'Instead of being daunted by the role of chance in genetic mutations as being the manifestation of

---

[5] David J. Bartholomew, *God of Chance* (London: SCM Press, 1984).

[6] A.R. Peacocke, 'Chance, Potentiality and God', *The Modern Churchman,* 17 (New Series 1973): 13-23; and in *Beyond Chance and Necessity,* ed. J. Lewis (London: Garnstone Press, 1974): 13-25; "Chaos or Cosmos", *New Scientist,* 63(1974): 386-389; A.R. Peacocke, *Creation and the World of Science* [henceforth *'CWS'*] (Oxford: Clarendon Press, 1979), chap. 3.

> irrationality in the universe, it would be more consistent with the observations to assert that the full gamut of the potentialities of living matter could be explored only through the agency of the rapid and frequent randomisation which is possible at the molecular level of DNA.'[7]

This role of 'chance', or rather randomness (or 'free experiment') at the micro-level is what one would expect if the universe were so constituted that all the potential forms of organisations of matter (both living and non-living) which it contains might be thoroughly explored. The interplay of chance and law is in fact creative within time, for it is the combination of the two which allows new forms to emerge and evolve - so that natural selection appears to be opportunistic. As in many games, the consequences of the fall of the dice depend very much on the rules of the game.[8] It has become increasingly apparent that it is chance operating within a law-like framework that is the basis of the inherent creativity of the natural order, its ability to generate new forms, patterns and organisations of matter and energy. If all were governed by rigid law, a repetitive and uncreative order would prevail: if chance alone ruled, no forms, patterns or organisations would persist long enough for them to have any identity or real existence - the universe could never be a cosmos and susceptible to rational inquiry. It is the combination of the two which makes possible an ordered

---

[7] *CWS*, p.94; see also by this author, *Theology for a Scientific Age: Being and Becoming-Natural, Divine and Human* [henceforth *TSA*] (SCM Press, London, 1993, 2nd enlarged edit.; repr. 1995), pp.115-121

[8] R. Winkler and M. Eigen, *Laws of the Game* (New York: Knopf, 1981. London: Allen Lane, 1982).

universe capable of developing within itself new modes of existence.

This combination, for a theist, can only be regarded as an aspect of the God-endowed features of the world. The way in which what we call 'chance' operates within this 'given' framework to produce new structures, entities and processes can then properly be seen as an eliciting of the potentialities that the physical cosmos possessed from the beginning. One might say that the potential of the 'being' of the world is made manifest in the 'becoming' that the operation of chance makes actual. God is the ultimate ground and source of both law ('necessity') and 'chance'.

To return to our musical model - for a theist, God must now be seen as acting, rather like the composer of a fugue, to create in the world ***through*** what we call 'chance' operating within the created order, each stage of which constitutes the launching pad for the next. The Creator, it now seems, is unfolding the divinely-endowed potentialities of the universe, in and through a process in which these creative possibilities and propensities (see next section), inherent by God's own intention within the fundamental entities of that universe and their inter-relations, become actualised within a created temporal development shaped and determined by those selfsame God-given potentialities.[9]

2.3 Trends in Evolution?

Given an immanentist understanding of God's presence 'in, with and under' the processes of biological evolution adopted up to this point, can God be said to be implementing any purpose in biological evolution? Or is the whole process so haphazard, such a matter of happenstance, such a matter of what Monod and Jacob called *bricolage*

[9] Cf., *CWS*, pp. 105-6 and *TSA*, pp.115-121.

(tinkering), that no meaning, least of all a divinely intended one, can be discerned in the process?

However there are propensities[10] in evolution towards the possession of certain characteristics, propensities that are inherently built into an evolutionary process based on natural selection of the best procreators. These properties naturally enhance survival for procreation in a wide range of environments. Thus it is that the evolutionary process is characterised by propensities towards increase in complexity, information-processing and storage, consciousness, sensitivity to pain, and even self-consciousness (a necessary prerequisite for social development and the cultural transmission of knowledge down the generations). *Some* successive forms, along *some* branch or 'twig' (à la Gould), have a distinct probability of manifesting more and more of these characteristics.[11] However, the actual physical form of

---

[10] Karl Popper has pointed out (in *A World of Propensities*, Thoemmes, Bristol, 1990) that the realisation of possibilities, which may be random, depend on the total situation within which the possibilities are being actualised so that "there exist weighted possibilities which are *more than mere possibilities*, but tendencies or propensities to become real" (p.12) and that these "propensities in physics are properties of *the whole situation* and sometimes even of the particular way in which a situation changes. And the same holds of the propensities in chemistry, in biochemistry, and in biology" (p.17).

[11] It is interesting to note that Richard Dawkins, too, in his *River Out of Eden* (London: Weidenfeld and Nicolson, 1995) includes (p.151ff.) amongst the thresholds that will be crossed *naturally* in a general chronology of a life explosion on any planet, anywhere in the universe ..... thresholds that any planetary replication bomb can be expected to pass',

the organisms in which these propensities are actualised and instantiated is contingent on the history of the confluence of disparate chains of events, including the survival of the mass extinctions that have occurred (96% of all species in the Permo-Triassic one[12]). So it is not surprising that recent re-interpretation of the fossils of very early (ca. 530 million years ago) soft-bodies fauna found in the Burgess shale of Canada show that, had any larger proportion of these survived and prevailed, the actual forms of contemporary, evolved creatures would have been very much more disparate in anatomical *plans* than those now observed to exist - albeit with a very great diversity in the few surviving designs.[13] But even had these particular organisms, unique to the Burgess shale, been the progenitors of subsequent living organisms, the same propensities towards complexity, etc., would also have been manifest in their subsequent evolution, for these 'propensities' simply reflect the advantages conferred in natural selection by these features. The same considerations apply to the arbitrariness and contingency of the mass extinctions, which Gould also strongly emphasises. So that, providing there had been enough time, a complex organism with consciousness, self-consciousness, social and cultural organisation (that is, the basis for the existence of 'persons') would have been likely eventually to have evolved and appeared on the Earth (or on some other planet amenable to the emergence of living organisms), though no doubt with a physical form very different from *Homo sapiens*. There can, it seems to me

---

those for: - high-speed information-processing (no. 5), achieved by possession of a nervous system; consciousness (no. 6, concurrent with brains); and language (no. 7).

[12] Gould, *Wonderful Life*, p.306, citing David M. Raup.

[13] Gould, *op.cit.*, p.49.

(*pace* Stephen Gould[14]) be overall direction and implementation of divine purpose through the interplay of chance and law without a deterministic plan fixing all the details of the structure(s) of what emerges possessing personal qualities. Hence the emergence of self-conscious persons capable of relating personally to God can still be regarded as an intention of God continuously creating through the processes of that to which he has given an existence of this contingent kind and not some other. It certainly must have been possible since it actually happened - with us!

I see no need to postulate any *special* action of God - along the lines, say, of some divine manipulation of mutations at the quantum level - to ensure that persons emerge in the universe, and in particular on Earth. To coin a phrase, 'I have no need of that hypothesis'![15]

---

[14] Gould, op.cit., p.51 and *passim*.

[15] If there are any such influences by God shaping the direction of evolutionary processes at specific points - for which I see no evidence (how could we know?) and no theological need - I myself could only envisage them as being through God's whole-part constraint on all-that-is affecting the confluence of what, to us, would be independent causal chains. Such specifically-directed constraints I would envisage as possible by being exerted upon the whole interconnected and interdependent system of the whole Earth in the whole cosmos which is in and present to God, who is therefore its ultimate Boundary Condition and therefore capable of shaping the occurrence of particular patterns of events, if God chooses to do so. For a fuller exposition of this approach, see *TSA*, pp. 157-165; and, more particularly and recently, 'God's Interaction with the World - The Implications of Derministic "Chaos" and of

2.4 The Diversity of Life

The natural world is immensely variegated in its hierarchies of levels of entities, structures and processes, in its 'being'; and abundantly diversifies with a cornucopian fecundity in its 'becoming' in time. From the unity in this diversity and the richness of the diversity itself, one may adduce[16] respectively, both the essential oneness of its source of being, namely the one God the Creator, and the unfathomable richness of the unitive Being of that Creator God. But now we must reckon more directly with the diversity itself. The forms even of non-living matter throughout the cosmos as it appears to us is even more diverse than what we can now observe immediately on the Earth. Furthermore the multiply branching tree of terrestrial biological evolution appears to be primarily opportunist in the direction it follows and, in so doing, produces the enormous variety of biological life on this planet. As Charles Darwin himself put it in a famous passage

> 'It is interesting to contemplate a tangled bank, clothed with many plants of many kinds, with birds singing on the bushes, with various insects flitting about, and with worms crawling through the damp earth, and to reflect that these elaborately constructed forms, so different from each other, and dependent upon each other in so complex a manner, have all been produced by laws acting around us...There is grandeur

---

Interconnected and Interdependent Complexity', in *Chaos and Complexity*, eds. R.J. Russell, N. Murphy and A.R. Peacocke (Vatican City State: Vatican Observatory Publications. Berkeley, California, U.S.A.: Centre for Theology and the Natural Sciences. 1995 - distributed by Univ. of Notre Dame Press.) 263-287.

[16] *TSA*, Chap. 8, section 1.

> in this view of life, with its several powers, having been originally breathed by the Creator into a few forms or into one; and that, whilst this planet has gone cycling on according to the fixed law of gravity, from so simple a beginning endless forms most beautiful and most wonderful have been, and are being evolved'.[17]

We can only conclude that, if there is a Creator, least misleadingly described in terms of 'personal' attributes, then that Creator intended this rich multiformity of entities, structures, and processes in the natural world and, if so, that such a Creator God takes what, in the personal world of human experience, could only be called 'delight' in this multiformity of what he has created. The existence of the *whole* tapestry of the created order, in its warp and woof, and in the very heterogeneity and multiplicity of its forms must be taken to be the Creator's intention. We can only make sense of that, utilising our resources of personal language, if we say that God has may be said to have something akin to 'joy' and 'delight' in creation. We have a hint of this in the satisfaction attributed to God as Creator in the first chapter of *Genesis*: 'And God saw everything he had made, and behold, it was very good'.[18] This naturally leads to the idea of the 'play' of God in creation on which I have expanded elsewhere,[19] in relation to Hindu thought as well as to that of Judaism and Christianity.

2.5 The Ubiquity of Pain, Suffering and Death

But now for the darker side.

The theist cannot ignore the ubiquity of pain, suffering and death as the necessary means of creation through biological

---

[17] C. Darwin, *The Origin of Species* (London: Thinkers Library, Watts, 6th edit.), p.408.

[18] *Genesis* 1,v.31.

[19] *CWS*, pp.108-111.

evolution. Any theodicy has to come to terms with the obliteration of far more species than now exist on the Earth. The spontaneity and fecundity of the biological world is gained at the enormous price of universal death and of pain and suffering during life.[20]

For any concept of God to be morally acceptable and coherent, if God is immanently present in and to natural processes then we cannot but infer that God suffers in, with and under the creative processes of the world with their costly unfolding in time. Rejection of the notion of the impassibility of God has, in fact, been a feature of the Christian theology of recent decades. There has been an increasing assent to the idea that it is possible

> 'to speak consistently of *a God who suffers eminently and yet is still God, and a God who suffers universally and yet is still present uniquely and decisively in the sufferings of Christ*'.[21]

As Paul Fiddes points out in his survey and analysis of this change in theological perspective, the factors that have promoted the view that God suffers are new assessments of 'the meaning of love [especially, the love of God], the implications of the cross of Jesus, the problem of [human] suffering, and the structure of the world'.[22] It is this last-mentioned - the 'structure of the world' - on which the new perspectives of the biological sciences bear by revealing the world processes to be such, as described above, that involvement in them by the immanent Creator has to be

---

[20] Cf., Dawkins' epithet, 'DNA neither cares nor knows. DNA just is. And we dance to its music' (*River out of Eden*, p.133).

[21] Paul S. Fiddes, *The Creative Suffering of God* (Oxford: Clarendon Press, 1988) p.3. (emphasis in the original).

[22] Ibid., p.45 (see also all of chap. 2).

regarded as involving suffering on the Creator's part. God, we find ourselves having to conjecture, suffers the 'natural' evils of the world along with ourselves because - we can but tentatively suggest at this stage - God purposes to bring about a greater good thereby, namely, the kingdom of free-willing, loving persons in communion with God and with each other.[23]

Because sacrificial, self-limiting, self-giving action on behalf of the good of others is, in human life, the hallmark of love, those who believe in Jesus the Christ as the self-expression of God's own self have come to see his life as their ultimate warrant for asserting that God is essentially 'Love', insofar as any one word can accurately refer to God's nature. Jesus' own teaching concerning God as 'Abba', Father, and of the conditions for entering the 'Kingdom of God' pointed to this too, but it was the person of Jesus and what happened to him that finally and early, established in the Christian community this perception of God as self-offering Love.

On their, and subsequent Christians', understanding Jesus the Christ is the definitive communication from God to humanity of the deep meaning of what God has been effecting in creation - and that is precisely what the Prologue to the Fourth Gospel says in terms of God the Word/*Logos*

---

[23] I hint here at my broad acceptance of John Hick's 'Irenaean' theodicy in relation to 'natural' evil (q.v., 'An Irenaean Theodicy', in *Encountering Evil*, ed. Stephen T. Davis (Edinburgh: T. & T. Clark, 1981), pp. 39-52; and his earlier *Evil and the God of Love* (London: Macmillan, 1966), especially chapters 15 and 16) and the position outlined by Brian Hebblethwaite in Chapter 5 ('Physical suffering and the nature of the physical world') in his *Evil, Suffering and Religion* (London: Sheldon Press, 1976).

as active in creation and as manifest in the person of Jesus the Christ.

As we saw, it may be inferred, however tentatively, from the character of the natural processes of creation that God has to be seen as suffering in, with and under these selfsame processes with their costly unfolding in time. But if God was present in and one with Jesus the Christ, then we have to conclude that *God* also suffered in and with him in his passion and death. The God whom Jesus therefore obeyed and expressed in his life and death is indeed a 'crucified God'[24] and the cry of dereliction can be seen as an expression of the anguish also of God in and through creation. If Jesus is indeed the self-expression of God in a human person, then the tragedy of his actual human life can be seen as a drawing back of the curtain to unveil a God suffering in and with the sufferings of created humanity and so, by natural extension, with those of all creation, since humanity is an evolved part of it. The suffering of God, which we could glimpse only tentatively in the processes of creation, is in Jesus the Christ concentrated into a point of intensity and transparency which reveals it to all who focus on him.

2.6 Human Evolution

That *Homo sapiens* represents only an extremely small, and very recently-arrived, fraction of living organisms that have populated the Earth raises the question of God's purposes in creating such a labrynth of life. To assume it was all there simply to lead to us clearly will not do. Hence the attribution to God of a sheer exuberance in creativity for its own sake, to which we have already referred. Moreover, since biological death was present on the Earth long before

---

[24] The title of Jurgen Moltmann's profound book, *The Crucified God* (London: SCM Press, 19743).

human beings arrived on the scene and was the pre-requisite of our coming into existence through the processes of biological evolution, when St. Paul says that "sin pays a wage, and the wage is death"[25] that cannot possibly mean for us now *biological* death. It can only mean 'death' in some other sense, such as the death of our relation to God consequent upon sin. I can see no sense in regarding biological death as the consequence of that very real alienation from God that is sin, because God had already used biological death as the means for creating new forms of life, including ourselves, long before we appeared on the Earth. This means those classical Christian formulations of the theology of the redemptive work of Christ that assume a causal connection between biological death and sin urgently need replacing.

The biological-historical evidence is that human nature has emerged only gradually by a continuous process from other forms of primates and that there are no sudden breaks of any substantial kind in the sequence noted by palaeontologists and anthropologists. Moreover there is *no* past period for which there is reason to affirm that human beings possessed moral perfection existing in a paradisal situation from which there has been only a subsequent decline. We appear to be rising beasts[26] rather than fallen angels! Although there was no golden age, no perfect past, no original perfect, individual "Adam" from whom all human beings have now declined, what *is* true is that humanity manifests aspirations to a perfection not yet attained, a potentiality not yet actualised, but no "original righteousness". Sin as alienation from God, humanity and nature is real and appears as the consequence

---

[25] *Rom.* 6 v. 23, REB.

[26] Rising from an a-moral (and in that sense) innocent state to the capability of moral, and immoral, action.

of our very possession of that *self*-consciousness which always places ourselves at the egotistical centre of our the 'universe' of our consciousness. Sin is about a falling short from what God intends us to be and is part and parcel of our having evolved into self-consciousness, freedom and intellectual curiosity. The domination of Christian theologists of redemption by classical conceptions of the 'Fall' urgently needs, it seems to me, to be rescinded and what we mean by redemption to be rethought if it is to make any sense to our contemporaries.

Now, we all have an awareness of the tragedy to fulfil our highest aspirations; of our failure to come to terms with finitude, death and suffering; of our failure to realise our potentialities and to steer our path through life. Freedom allows us to make the wrong choices, so that sin and alienation from God, from our fellow human beings and from nature are real features of our existence. So the questions of not only "Who are we?" but, even more acutely, "What should we be becoming - where should we be going?" remain acute for us. To be brief, I find the clue to the answers to these questions in the person of Jesus of Nazareth and what he manifested of God's perennial expression in creation (as the *Logos* of God incarnate). Hence I am impelled to consider specifically Christian affirmations in the light of the foregoing re-considerations of God's creating through an evolutionary process.

3. The significance of Jesus the Christ in a possible Christian evolutionary perspective

"..[I]n scientific language, the Incarnation may be said to have introduced a new species into the world - the Divine man transcending past humanity, as humanity transcended the rest of the animal creation, and communicating His vital energy by a spiritual process to subsequent

generations..." (J.R. Illingworth, in the 12th edition of *Lux Mundi*, 1891, p.132.)

Jesus' resurrection demonstrated to the disciples, notably to Paul, and now to us, that it is the union of *his* kind of life with God which is not broken by death and capable of being taken up into God. For he manifested the kind of human life which can become fully life with God, not only here and now, but eternally beyond the threshold of death. Hence his imperative "Follow me" now constitutes for us a call for the transformation of humanity into a new kind of human being and becoming. What happened to him, Jesus saw *could* happen to all.

In this perspective, Jesus the Christ, the whole Christ event, has shown us what is possible for humanity. The actualisation of this potentiality can properly be regarded as the consummation of the purposes of God already incompletely manifested in evolving humanity. In Jesus there was a *divine* act of new creation because the initiative was *from God* within human history, within the responsive human will of Jesus inspired by that outreach of God into humanity designated as 'God the Holy Spirit'. Jesus the Christ is thereby seen, in the context of the whole complex of events in which he participated (the 'Christ event'), as the paradigm of what God intends for all human beings, now revealed as having the potentiality of responding to, of being open to, of becoming united with, God.

The death and resurrection of Jesus as manifesting uniquely that quality of life which can be taken up by God into the fullness of God's own life implicitly involves an affirmation about what the basic potentiality of all humanity is. It shows us that, regardless of our particular human skills and creativities - indeed regardless of almost all that the social mores of our times applauds - it is through a radical openness to God, a thoroughgoing self-offering love for others and for God's creation, and obedience to God, that we grow into such communion with the eternal God that *God* does not allow biological death to rupture that potentially timeless relation. Irenaeus, in accord with the Eastern Christian tradition, says it all:

> "The Word of God, our Lord Jesus Christ
> Who of his boundless love
> became what we are
> to make us what even he himself is."[27]

[27] Irenaeus, *Adv.Haer.*, v, praef.

THE EVOLUTION OF RELIGION

Rev. Dr. Clinton Bennett

Lecturer, Westminster College Oxford

Introduction: A Post-modern Inquiry

Two preliminary points. First, I have adopted a post-modern model of inquiry in this paper, as I address the questions: how did the religious dimension of human culture begin, and has it evolved through various phases of development. Second, because of my own rootedness within a religion, I shall conclude this paper by suggesting a theology of religions. Postmodernity has alerted us to the manipulative element in our construction of reality. What were once taken to be truths, norms, realities, historical and even scientific facts, actually reflect the agendas, biases, interests, and personal preferences, of those who occupied the centres of power at the time that these norms were established, or that these truths were asserted. Michel Foucault (1926-84) has shown how any discourse, whether historical, anthropological, psychological, or scientific, is produced by a process of choosing one method of selecting, or of classifying data, over other methods. Whatever is left out is lost. Foucault went so far as to say that there is no such thing as abstract truth, no transcendent reality, only what you and I construe. If this is so, then rights and wrongs, normality and abnormality, definitions of sanity, insanity, health, sickness and so on, are the social and political constructs of the powerful. Many may have been devised to control the population:

> "Generally speaking, all the authorities exercising individual control function according to a double mode (mad/sane, dangerous/harmless, normal/abnormal) and that of coercive assignment, of differential distribution; how he is to be recognised; how constant surveillance is to be exercised over him" (Foucault, 1979 p.199).

The object here may be the criminal, or the madman/women, or the sexually or indeed the religiously deviant. Postmodernity tends to critique the notion of sameness, and to rejoice instead in difference, in diversity. Postmodern writers have been described as characteristically hybrid - often this is true of their own backgrounds, as well as of their literary creations; Timothy Mo, Kazuo Ishiguro, Salman Rushdie, for example. Postmodernity, says Professor Akbar Ahmed (1992) "allows, indeed encourages, the juxtaposition of discourses, as exuberant eclecticism, the mixing of diverse images" (p.25). Of course, taken too far, this results in a very pessimistic view of the human reality. Meaningful discourse *between* people may become problematic. If I create my world, you yours, dialogue between us may be impossible. However, in my view, we can no longer ignore the possibility that our meta-narratives may not be as authoritative, as factual, or as true, as we once thought they were; rather, they may reflect *and protect* the interests of the powerful over the powerless. Or my interests over yours, and so on. Once the Roman Emperors, converted to Christianity, had convened and chaired the councils which construed Christian doctrinal correctness, any one who dissented from the creeds became not only a heretic, but also a dangerous political and social deviant who had to be punished, and from whom the rest of the populace had to be protected.

Post-modernity and the Study of Religion

Applied to theological discourse, or to an exploration of the religious dimension of human culture, postmodernity poses some fundamental questions. For example, can any claim to be universally true, and valid, be sustained? Christian missionaries have gone forth unto the nations of the earth, proclaiming that Christianity alone is true, and the only path to salvation. Other religions are false, or misguided, and must be abandoned. This claim to absolute truth is in turn connected with the claim that there *is* an ultimate Truth, with a capital "T", which Christians call "God", which has determined goodness and badness, normality and abnormality, and so on. These are not social or political constructs, subject to change but are eternal and immutable, just like God. Thus, a postmodern, and a religious world-view, may operate with quite different assumptions. On the one hand, however, post-modernity allows any one to construe whatever world-view they want to - including religious world-views. On the other, it critiques any claim to exclusivity; asserting difference, not sameness.

But where does this leave us in terms of our task, which is to explore the evolution of religion? One: it warns us that whatever has been said about the origin, or function, or indeed about the future of religion, or about one religion's status over-and-against others, inevitably reflects the agenda of the speaker. Two: it invites us to examine critically what religions claim *about* themselves. Some claim to have dropped ready made out of heaven, and do not regard themselves as products of an evolutionary process at all. The degree to which any evolutionary, or developmental theory of religion, clashes with a religion's self-understanding, needs to be noted. This may create a real dilemma for any student of religion who wants to claim, on the *one* hand, to be an objective scholar operating, broadly speaking, within the social sciences, who also, on the other hand, wants to take seriously what religious people say about their religion.

The Study of Religion: A Value Free Science?

The pioneer students of religion were anxious to establish a distinctive identity for themselves, which would distinguish them from those who wrote about religion with a polemical, or missionary, or apologetic, brief. Instead, they would be descriptive, value-free social scientists. They would observe and categorise, collect data on religious beliefs and practices, and so on, without passing any judgement on the ultimate significance, truth, or otherwise, of what they studied. Even so, they *were* making certain assumptions about the subject matter of their study. For example, in categorising the Qur'an, and the Bible, and the Vedas, as "scriptures", they were assuming that they were comparing like with like, dealing with *different* examples of the *same* phenomenon. This assumption would be debated by some religious people; some Hindus say that the Vedas are the truest scriptures, that the Christian Gospels are absurd and lack truthfulness. Some Christians say that the Qur'an was composed by Muhammad, whereas the Bible was inspired by God. Thus, one book has a human origin, and is flawed, whilst the other has a divine origin, and is incomparable with any other so-called scripture. There is no *universal* category called "scripture", into which different texts can be slotted; rather, there is *one* Scripture, and many other texts which purport to be scripture. Theology of religions addresses this theological battle-ground; the study of religion has generally avoided developing a general theory about religion. In her book, *A History of God* (1993) Karen Armstrong pointed out that what she was writing was not a history of "the ineffable reality of God, which is beyond time and change, but a history of the way in which men and women have perceived him" (p.4.). Similarly, the study of religion has concerned itself with studying religious beliefs and practices as a dimension of human culture without attempting to evaluate the truthfulness of any particular theological claim. In fact, the idea that God is ineffable, beyond time and change, and is a "he", is itself a human notion. Process theology offers an alternative understanding of God. However, if the study of *religion* implies that all religious beliefs and practices are expressions of a single phenomenon out there, then the "study of *religions*", which may be the preferred name for the discipline, makes no such assumption. We may be studying phenomen<u>a</u> not a phenomen<u>o n</u>.

In fact, the problem of finding a suitable name for itself - comparative religion, or the scientific study of religion, the study of religion, or the study of religion<u>s</u>, or Religious Studies are all amongst the candidates - is as challenging as that of defining exactly what its subject matter is! Clifford Geertz (1968) put it like this, "The comparative study of religion has always been plagued by this peculiar embarrassment; the elusiveness of its subject matter" (p.1). Eric Sharpe (1983) wrote;

> Definitions of religion, in a sense, remind one of the fable of the blind men attempting to define an elephant. One touches its trunk and describes it as a snake, another touches its ear and describes it as a winnowing-fan; another touches its leg and describes it as a tree; another its tail and describes it as a broom (p.46).

Sharpe goes on to suggest that although we can not definitively define religion, we nevertheless *recognise* it when we see it, in a common sense sort of way. Thus, we can draw up a list of the type of things we take to be religious, and categorise them accordingly when we stumble across them. We may not be studying anything that is in any way connected with an ultimate Truth, or reality; we are studying what human beings do, and have done - they pray, they worship, they produce sacred artefacts, they draw up doctrinal statements, they organise themselves into religious fraternities. And, they have claimed that all this activity gives their life meaning and purpose; that it enhances the quality of human living. As Karen Armstrong suggests, it is because this has been such an enduring feature of human experience that what we call religion merits study. We can also add to the above: people have *argued* about their religious beliefs, they have even shed blood as a result of religious claims.

Religion's Origin

What mainly concerns us in the context of this Consultation are theories about the origin, and development, or evolution, of religion. These, generally, have been formed by scholars whose primary location was in disciplines other than Religious Studies - by psychologists, theologians, anthropologists, scientists, sociologists, and so on - because, as I have laboured somewhat, Religious Studies has been descriptive. Turning now to some of these theories, I shall argue that they inevitably reflect the *a priori* assumptions of their proposers. This is *my* post-modern diagnosis. Looking down the deep, and murky, well of history, scholars have glimpsed at the bottom a pale reflection of their own image; that is, of their own world-view. Theories about the origin, and evolution, of religion, can be grouped into three different sets; some define religion as a human cultural or social or psychological construct. From the religious point of view, these theories are reductionist. They subtract the *religious* from religion. In other words, they reject the reality of any divine or ineffable or ultimate or universal or eternal or transcendent or immanent, or immanent and transcendent, Truth. Their evaluation of religion may be either positive, or negative, depending upon their agenda. Its origin, however, like dance, or art, or politics - is human. Other theories endorse the claim, made by religions, that they are not merely human constructs but the product of a supra-human reality. Usually, such theories are positive about the value of religion, although they may well recognise that it can be subject to abuse. These two sets of theories tend to assume that when we discuss Islam, Judaism, Christianity, and so on, we are dealing with comparable phenomena - or indeed with a single phenomenon, that of religion. Theories under my third heading, theological theories, may claim that one religion is true, others false, or that some religions are truer than others; or that all are relatively true. Such theories may be possible to classify within one of my first two groups; however, they certainly do not all assume that everything "religious" is really religious. They do, though, assert, the truthfulness of their own ultimate religious claims, often over-and-against other peoples' claims.

In this paper, I am not going to attempt a detailed exploration of all the available theories. Some I have discussed at greater length, and in more depth, in my book, *In Search of.The Sacred* (1996). Some I shall summarise here. Some I have not dealt with - either in my book, or in this paper. What I offer is selective; and my selection is offered in order to argue a thesis. Postmodernity, I believe, allows me to do this, but it also invites me to be frank and open about my thesis, so here it is. No single theory of religion can command unqualified support. Theories which stress negative aspects of religion, and theories which are positive about the value of religion can usefully be brought into dialogue with each other. Human-origin theories remind us that there is always a human element in religion. Supra-human origin theories challenge us to ask whether we *are* the sum of our own knowledge; and, even if we cannot prove that we are, or are not, the persistence of belief in the supra-human may liberate me, personally (indeed it does) to persist in my own God-belief until I am convinced that my belief is delusive. Since I have no way to make sense of the world without using the particular hermeneutic which I happen to prefer, I shall continue to construe reality accordingly - and conclude this paper by telling you what this does for me. This, I repeat, is my post-modern diagnosis. At this conference, which addresses the over-arching question, "Evolution, or How Did We Get Here?" it is certainly germane to point out that many origin of religion theories have been influenced by evolutionary thought. Let me, therefore, start some of these.

Human-origin theories

An early theorist of religion was James George Frazer, 1854-1941, the UK's very first professor of social anthropology. He had it that religion replaced magic, and is in its turn replaced by science, as human beings struggle to understand how the world works. Magic attempted to control nature either sympathetically, or contagiously; sympathy assumes that like influences like, contagion that what has been in contact with something else may carry on influencing that object even when separated. Magic gives way to religion when people realise their inability to control, or to explain, the world, that they have been "pulling at strings to which nothing has been attached" (ed. 1994 p.55). The rain-dance, the fertility-dance, enjoy no link with cloud, or with sperm-egg.! When this truth dawns on us, we begin to think that maybe "some other beings", like us "but far stronger" direct the elements; and what we have to do is to serve them. This results in religion. Later, belief in the many deities yields to belief in "one supreme creator and controller of all things" (1926 p.9). Religious institutions, rituals, artefacts, and so on, evolve to service the worship of the Creator. Later still, religion yields to science. Science ultimately wins out over magic and religion because it is evolutionally superior - empirical facts will replace superstition. Science, unlike religion, places us exactly where we are placed; neither totally able, nor unable, to shape our destiny but aided in the attempt to do so only by our own intelligence. Magic, although wrong, was better than religion because it at least saw us as active agents, not as passive objects, in the business of ordering the cosmos.

Frazer was himself a devout Presbyterian. However, whilst there may been room in his theory for some historical dialectic - making the magic, religion, science progression inevitable - it had no room for a superintending God. It made God redundant. Religion, as an opting out of responsibility, belongs to an evolutionary primitive stage of human development. Frazer's theory is a good example of what I have called "human origin theories" because it has much in common with other influential and important theories of this genre. For example, with Sigismund Freud (1856-1939), for whom religion results from a projection of our hopes and fears, dreams and nightmares, onto an imaginary father-figure, who will make it all right in the end. Religion, for Freud, was also a type of psychological malady; and, like all maladies, it had a sexual basis. Here we see how a scholar who claimed scientific status for his work, convinced from the outset that all psychosis has a sexual link, found in his data the evidence he needed to prove this theses. This, of course, does not mean that Freud was wrong, that the evidence was not there. Perhaps it was. However, alerted to Freud's thesis that sex would be there, we may not be post-modernly surprised to learn that he discovered it to be there. Religion, in this view, is a malady, an illusion, a residue of human infancy not a mark of human maturity; and has not future. Again, it is science which will reveal its inadequacy. Religion, alongside science, will simply not be the fittest - and so will not survive. Frazer's and Freud's *a priori* assumptions, though, are clear; only science can unlock life's mysteries; religion sooner or later, will be abandoned as a childlike, if not as a childish delusion.

Supra-human origin theories: can perhaps be best represented by Carl Jung (1865-1961), Freud's erstwhile disciple, indeed heir apparent. Jung harps on incessantly about the scientific status of his research. However, his theory of religion contrasts in almost every respect with that of his former mentor. Jung disagreed with Freud about the sexual basis of all maladies; nor did he think religion was a malady. Instead, he developed the theory that there really is a God-reality; and, in all of us, there resides a "god-image". This is not a primitive projection - but our response to the archetypal *numina*,. or God. This "god-image" has passed into the collective unconscience, and continues to inform the religious dimension of human life alongside other dimensions. This is a type of biological sub-stratum, a psychic-reality, as real as the biological, even as real as the scientific. Jung, though, appears to have thought that this dimension always resulted in human good; he seems to have neglected what has been called the "dark side of religion". I return to this in a minute or two.

Alister Hardy, whose legacy the Religious Experience Research Centre here at Westminster College preserves, similarly held that the religious is a type of biological stratum of human life, as real as other dimensions - and links us with a God-reality. Religious experience manifests this reality. Quite a few religions may have very little quarrel with this theory. Islam, for example, could well be happy with the idea that Mohammed underwent genuine religious experiences, through which God revealed God's will, Islam, for human life. On the other hand, Mohammed's, and other peoples' religious experiences, have been dismissed as self-induced, as psychotic - Islam has been explained away as a clever system of social control created by the ingenuity of its founder. Karl Marx's theory of religion posits that it represents the opium of the people; an instrument whereby the rich and powerful can keep the poor and the enslaved passive and obedient, but hardworking *today*, with the promise of reward after death.

The "religious experience" theory is sometimes used as a trump-card, to prove that religion is what it claims to be over-and-against its detractors. However, neuro-psychologist Michael Persinger has isolated the "temporal lobe" as the source of such experiences - and says that seismic activity sets off atmospheric reactions which in turn stimulate unusual activity in the lobe (see Cotton, 1995). Thus, an experience such as Mohammed's can be explained biologically; and may have had no connection whatsoever with anything like a God-type reality. On the other hand, even if Persinger is right, and the temporal lobe is where religious experience is as it were biologically located; this does not prove that God does not cause the seismic activity which stimulates the lobe's reaction at just the right moment. A sceptical hermeneutic may find the evidence convincing; a hermeneutic of faith, convinced that Mohammed's experiences were genuinely religious, and that religious experiences respond to divine stimulus, will find the evidence wanting. And so on.

Theological Theories: Here, briefly, are two. I take both from the Christian tradition but their equivalents may be found elsewhere. Lesslie Newbigin, who once taught me missiology, argues that the Cross and Resurrection of Christ are to be taken as historical facts. Taken thus, he says, it follows that:

> "If, in fact, it is true that almighty God, creator and sustainer of all that exists in heaven and on earth, has - at a known time and place in human history - so humbled himself as to become part of our sinful humanity and to suffer and die a shameful death to take away our sin and to rise from the dead as the first-fruit of a new creation; if this is a fact, then to affirm it is no arrogance. To remain quiet about it is treason to our fellow human beings ... One can, of course, deny the story. One can say it is not fact but legend. But if it is fact it cannot be slotted into some way of understanding the world based on other presuppositions, it can only be the starting-point, the pre-supposition of all our struggle to understand the world, including our struggle to understand the world of history" (1988 p.328).

Newbigin argues for an exclusive theology of religions - salvation is through Christ, because in Christ God has acted, as he has acted in no other way, and no where else, to redeem humanity. Of course, one may argue that humanity needs no redeemer - that she/he must redeem her/himself, and so on. Newbigin does not say that other religions contain nothing that came from God - or that only those who explicitly profess Christian faith will get into heaven; he does say that Christ alone is the vehicle of salvation. In a sense, evolution has no place within this world-view. Religion as it were, comes from without the evolution process - if indeed there is one.

My second theology of religions is the pluralism of writers such as John Hick. For Hick, there *is* an Ultimate Reality, but this has not definitively or exclusively revealed itself through a single religion. Rather, located within particular different cultural, historical, social contexts, people *apprehend* this Reality. No apprehension is absolute. All are partial. Some, though, may be better than others at enhancing the quality of human life, which Hick takes to be purpose of all religion. Some are better at placing generosity and self-less-ness at the centre; thus replacing the human ego as the hub around which all else revolves. This could mean that the religion best suited to this task will one day displace all others.

Perhaps a new religion, the religion of the future, drawing on the best aspects of many religions, will evolve. Hick himself doesn't advocate this. Nor does he advocate a grading of religions - this would involve too many assumptions about worth, value, making judgements about other people's worldviews, each the product of its own context. The diversity of human cultures will continue, he thinks, to require religious pluralism. We will need, however, to revise our exclusive doctrines. In another sense, Hick's world-view, like that of many religious people, may have a bone to pick with any evolutionary theory that sees the survival of the fittest as the human norm. Religious placing of the Other at the centre means that the weak and the vulnerable, who are not the physically or even the intellectually fittest, are yet to be valued. Hick's worldview, whilst upholding the reality of the Ultimate - which may be viewed as a personal God, or as impersonal Truth, and so on, also takes the human element of religion seriously. Religious systems, beliefs, practices, are all products of human, and partial, responses. None have ultimate value; all can therefore be modified. This contrasts with the view, for example, that what the Pope says *ex cathedra* is infallible, or that what the councils of the church determined were divinely guided truths. Also, since one modifies, I suppose, in order to improve, it runs counter to the belief that what we already have is perfect, or nearly so.

Towards a Postmodern religious world-view:

The more I study other people's religions, and other people's theories about how they may have got to where they are today - as a Durkheimian social consensus on values, or as a Marxist system of social control, or as a Freudian illusion, or as a Frazerian opting out of responsibility, or as a human response to the ineffable, and so on, the more I become convinced that there is much in all of this that I must take seriously. I have been criticised by one reviewer for "playing down the role of power and control in any religious organisation" - the so-called "dark side of religion" (Gellner, 1996). It is this to which Marxist theory alerts us. And this must be taken seriously. The element of corruption, of failing to live up to our ideals, must be acknowledged within all our religious, indeed within all our human institutions, social, political, and cultural. The degree to which religion does represent an opting out, perhaps stifling human inventivity, similarly needs to be acknowledged. At the cutting edge of embryonic, and of other medical research, there are real issues here which must be explored. However, it is as someone personally sympathetic to religious belief that I derive both these critiques from theories of religion which have been un-sympathetic towards religion. Religions which stress human ability to change, and to change for the better, may constructively be set alongside those that stress human waywardness. Perhaps the truth lies somewhere between the two. My conclusion, then, is that we need to hold all these theories, even those which appear to be directly confrontational, in creative tension with each other.

This, I suggest, is what post-modernism invites. I cannot reject any theory out of hand, even if I dislike the particular set of *a priori* assumptions which aided the thesis along the way. I happen to have my own set, disliked by some, liked by others. What post-modernism challenges us to do is to find ways of *allowing* cultural and social and religious diversity, whilst preventing clashes between them. Its political agenda has been described thus:

> "The unanswered question at the heart of the postmodern political agenda is how to make a common cause to preserve difference, how to create a sense of solidarity that will be both 'more expansive ... than we presently have' " (Rorty, 1989 p.196) and "conducive to the preservation and enhancement of difference" (Smart, 1993 p.105).

The religious agenda is, I think, somewhat similar: how can we enhance our acceptance of difference whilst yet making common cause to ensure that we, and the planet we occupy, not only survive but also flourish. I posit this because there is considerable evidence that this is the point to which our religions have brought us, even if we are not quite certain how. My whole adult life has been committed to inter-religious dialogue; there is a speaking together today, made possible by the global village, that could not, and did not, to any significant degree, happen before. Hans Kung, and others, are promoting a global ethical initiative - since, as Paul Knitter puts it in his latest book, "in order to foster the well being of persons *in this world*, we will have *to change* this world ... for it is painfully evident [that] so many practices and structures of nations and of the international community [and, I want to add, of religions, including my own] are death-dealing rather than life-giving for millions of people" (1997 p.116). Religion, on the one hand, is responsible for some of the ills of our world; on the other hand, it does give people hope, and it *may* enable them to change things for the better. Nor does religion seem to be dying out - as many thinkers have predicted. There may be a decline in membership of mainstream Churches, for example, but there is also a proliferation of religious ways of construing reality, new age, alternative religious movements, and so on. It seems to me that even if my God-belief is, at the end of the day, falacious - if it helps me to be a better person, and to help others, then it fulfils a positive function. This reminds me of Auguste Compte's Positivist Church (see Bennett, 1996 p.26). If, on the other hand, it does none of this, it ought to be abandoned. If we religious people can find ways of affirming difference, yet work together for the common good, and if, instead of merely predicting the future, we also take steps to help to shape it - religion may evolve into a life-enhancing, post-modern, liberating, perspective on life, on the planet, and on the Cosmos beyond it. If it is predetermined, by the dialectic of nature, or by its own inherent weakness, that religion dies out, it will. But if religious people rise to the moment in which they find themselves, religion may yet prove to be a mark of human maturity, not a residue of our infancy, best left, like our childhood toys, behind us. We need to be aware, though, that what we religiously conceive to be positive, may be dubbed retrogressive by others. It may be argued that a world free of the less-able, or of certain races, or of particular groups of people - for example, would be a better world in which the fit would become even fitter, the strong even stronger. As I have suggested, religion critiques some views of what is good for the human species.

References (cited and consulted).

Ahmed, Akbar (1992) *postmodernism and Islam: Predicament and Promise*, London, Routledge.

Armstrong, Karen (1993) *A History of God*, London, Mandarin

Bennett, Clinton (1996) *In Search of the Sacred: Anthropology and the Study of Religions*, London, Cassell

Cotton, Ian (1995) *The Hallelujah Revolution*, London, Little, Brown and Co.

Cox, Harvey (1988) *Many Mansions*, London, Collins

Frazer, James George (1926) *The Worship of Nature*, Edinburgh, Gifford Lectures

Foucault, Michel (1977) *Discipline and Punish*, London, Allen Lane

Frazer, James George (ed. 1994) *The Golden Bough*, London, OUP.

Freud, Sigismund (1928, ed. 1978) *The Future of An Illusion*, London, Hogarth Press

Geertz, Clifford (1968) *Islam Observed*, Chicago, The University Press

Gellner, David N. (1996) "Review of C. Bennett's *In Search of the Sacred"*, *Discernment*, ns Vol. 1, no. 3, pp.11-24.

Jung, Carl (1971) *The Portable Jung*, Harmondsworth, Penguin

Knitter, Paul (1997) *Jesus and Other Names: Christian Mission and Global Responsibility*, Oxford, Oneworld

Newbigin, Lesslie, (1989) *The Gospel in a Pluralist Society*, London, SPCK

Rorty, R. (1979) *Philosophy and the Mirror of Nature*, Princeton, Princeton University Press

Sharpe, Eric J. (1983) *Understanding Religion*, London, Duckworth

Smart, Barry (1993) *Postmodernity: Key Ideas*, London, Routledge

CHAIRMAN'S CONCLUSIONS

Professor Alec Garner

I cannot hope to do anything like justice to the several lectures we have heard over the last two days by way of either comment or summary, and I shall not try. Rather I will briefly mention a facet of biological evolution which complements the competitive forces dominant in Darwinian theory.

Evolutionary theory is still perceived by many both in the Church and in science to be a rebuttal of religion and it has been salutary to be put in possession of the facts by speakers who have spoken with authority and understanding. So far from necessarily undermining faith we have seen that the evolutionary process can, with equal validity, be interpreted as the way in which God achieves his creative purpose. What we have tried to do in this consultation was to look at our origins and confront the question of how it is that we have come to be what we are, to ask with the psalmist "What is man?......... Thou hast made him a little lower than the angels!"

From an ancestry shared in some measure with the simplest bacteria we have emerged as creatures able to apprehend the One who created us. How? Starting with a consideration of the biological evolutionary process as first clearly described by Darwin we were then introduced to a more detailed examination of our presumed roots as human beings. Next we saw the emergence of culture as the dominant factor in our development, a development that had to await that most profound mystery, the emergence of consciousness. Hardly less enigmatic and miraculous has been the origin of language, as Professor Clark pointed out. Then the supreme mystery of evolution, surely its pinnacle, our ability to relate to the Divine.

Survival, at the biological level at least, can be a struggle with the weakest going under. Once we emerged as sentient creatures capable of intelligent mutual interaction, co-operation became an increasingly essential element in that survival process with its apogee a capacity for altruism and self-sacrifice of which Christ Jesus is the exemplar.

But a capacity for co-operation appears to have been integral to biological life as well from the earliest multicellular organisms some 600-700 million years ago. Thus, not all cells in such an organism perform the same function. There are a variety of cells with very different activities - brain cells, liver cells, muscle cells and so on - and yet all have the same complement of genes which is to say the same initial potential. The differences arise because only a proportion of those genes are functional and the active genes in a brain cell, say, are not the same as those triggered in a liver cell. Much remains to be explained as to what turns some genes on in one cell and another set in a second cell, but of undoubted importance are chemical signals emanating form the various cells. To put it simply, the cells talk to one another. This expression of certain capabilities with suppression of others for the benefit of the organism as a whole is not quite in line with a concept of evolution based solely on competition. It speaks, as one of our members has put it, of "nature green in cell and leaf"[1] not just "red in tooth and claw"[2]

There is another facet of the evolutionary process that deserves attention. The mutations that provide grist for the mill of incremental changes in a cell's capability are apparently random. But there may be more to it than that, and it is conceivable that the seemingly chance mutations operate within a set of constraints serving to increase the possibility of a productive outcome. An analogy, courtesy of Lewis Carroll[3], may help. If we set out to convert the three-letter word PIG to STY changing one letter at a time on a purely random basis, given the twenty-six letters in the alphabet, it could take up to 17,000 moves without even allowing for repeats of the various combinations. Should we, however, impose a set of rules such that each combination must make literary sense for it to be accepted the conversion becomes much more probable. It can be achieved in just six moves:

PIG –> WIG –> WAG –> WAY –> SAY –> STY

Similarly, natural selection insists that a mutation must make biological sense for it to be perpetuated, in that it is compatible with continued survival. It may take many throws of the dice before an acceptable mutation occurs. One biologist[4] writes: "Evolution proceeds by short phases of rapid change separated by long periods of stasis.........Chance still plays a role, but within a set of constraints so stringently limiting the range of possibilities..........that evolving systems have to wait many millions of years for the dice to fall inside the allowed boundaries". Nevertheless, he goes on to say, " ..... the history of life on Earth allows less leeway to contingency and unpredictability than current fashion claims." Suggested constraints have to do with such things as the nature of the component materials of living organisms, the environment in which they interact, and time factors. It is interesting to note what Darwin, himself, had to say: "I am inclined to look at everything as resulting from designed laws, with the details, whether good or bad, left to the working out of what we may call chance........I cannot think that the world as we see it is the result of chance; yet I cannot look at each separate thing as the result of design". Chance with constraints or a loaded dice. Theoretically it is conceivable that as complicated a structure as an eye could have developed as the result of a large number of fortuitous mutations (in the order of several thousands). On the other hand eyes, despite their complexity and correspondingly massive odds against their emergence, have developed not once but several times in distinct lineages in the course of evolution, each version having evolved separately and not as a variation on a single prototype. This is hard to explain on the basis of a chance sequence that has so many odds stacked against it. An alternative view which accords with this observation more successfully is that there is an organising principle that all but guarantees that certain structures, such as the eye, will form.

Might I suggest then that evolution, which we have no reason to think has come to an end, even at a purely biological level, and certainly not in cultural or religious terms, is a product of co-operation and design as well as competition and chance. In which case a supreme accolade for us as sentient creatures whom 'He has made a little lower than the angels' is to be, as Dr. Peacocke[5] has put it, co-creators with God in the continuing evolutionary process.

References

[1] John Barnes. Nature Green in Cell and Leaf. Quaker Universalist Pamphlet No.14, London, 1994.

[2] Alfred Tennyson. In Memoriam. 1850.

[3] Lewis Carroll. Cited by S.Jones, The Language of the Genes, p.147. Harper Collins, London, 1993.

[4] Christian de Duve. Vital Dust: The Origin of life on Earth, p.296. BasicBooks, New York, 1995.

[5] Arthur R. Peacocke. Theology for a Scientific Age, p.343. SCM, London, 1993.

SERMON

Rev. Professor C. Kingsley Barrett
Professor Emeritus of Divinity, Durham University

Evolution

Therefore as sin came into the world through one man and death through sin, and so death spread to all men because all men sinned - sin indeed was in the world before the law was given, but sin is not counted where there is no law. Yet death reigned from Adam to Moses, even over those whose sins were not like the transgression of Adam, who was a type of the one who was to come. But the free gift is not like the trespass. For if many died through one man's trespass, much more have the grace of God and the free gift in the grace of that one man Jesus Christ abounded for many. And the free gift is not like the effect of that one man's sin. For the judgment following one trespass brought condemnation, but the free gift following many trespasses brings justification. If, because of one man's trespass, death reigned through that one man, much more will those who receive the abundance of grace and the free gift of righteousness reign in life through the one man Jesus Christ. Then, as one man's trespass led to condemnation for all men, so one man's act of righteousness leads to acquittal and life for all men. For as by one man's disobedience many were made sinners, so by one man's obedience many will be made righteous. Law came in, to increase the trespass; but where sin increased, grace abounded all the more, so that, as sin reigned in death, grace also might reign through righteousness to eternal life through Jesus Christ our Lord.

Romans 5:12-21

To choose this text for this occasion might seem like an intended provocation. "You may spend a couple of days talking about evolution if you like, but at the end we are going back to the old story of creation - Adam and Eve and the Garden of Eden. Away with Darwin and his evolution; we have no apes for our grandfathers." Of course, it is no such thing, neither in its original intention nor in mine. It is probably true that Paul read the opening chapters of Genesis in a way rather different from ours, and with no reference to Big Bangs or other fashionable accounts of creation. But anyone can see that in this paragraph Adam, whatever else he may have been, is primarily a theological - or anthropological - concept, comparable with and standing over against the other great theological concept, Christ. Paul has no interest in telling a tale, passing on a legend, of creation. He is talking about humanity, related as it is about the two poles, the two universal and representative men, Adam and Christ. In any case, it is not creation but how we get from creation to here, that he is dealing with, and that process is, more or less, evolution. How did human beings, and the non-human beings who are our neighbours, and how did human and other institutions and activities, become what we know, or think we know, them to be now?

I am a theologian, with some scientific roots in mathematics, and no knowledge of the life-sciences at all, and it seems to me, looking from the outside, that evolutionary theory has evolved a good deal since Darwin's time; certainly it has been applied - not always, I think, convincingly - in a great variety of fields. But I am beginning with what I understand to be basic Darwinism, by which I mean evolution proceeding by means of natural selection; and with Paul's guidance I hope to see something of its theological and practical significance.

The basic proposition from which I begin - we shall come to the text in due course - is that Darwinism is a demythologised version of the doctrine of original sin. But I think I had better define my terms.

Original sin means that there is something wrong with the human race; not just with this or that member of it, though we all share in it, but with the race as a whole. It is at least in part a corporate concept. Nothing makes the wrongness clearer than does the old myth of Adam and Eve, the snake and the apple. Adam and Eve wanted to possess the desirable object - the fruit was "to be desired". They wanted it because they believed that it was the way to power over their environment, in the end, power over God. The tree was the tree of knowledge, and knowledge is what you need to gain power over your environment - knowledge of how to make a wheel, knowledge of how to use electro-magnetic radiation and control genetic processes. "And", said the snake, "Eat and you will have knowledge, eat and you will be like God, on his level, no longer his subordinates." So man has a will-to-power; no harm in that if he will use it rightly. The snake persuades him to use it wrongly.

The will-to-power can be abused in any part of life; it constantly is abused in the field of religion. That is why I asked that Genesis 4 should be read as the lesson, rather than Genesis 3. Here we have two brothers, Cain and Abel, and they are both religious men; that is, they both want to be in with God. But one of them has found out that animal sacrifice works better than vegetable. So what is poor Cain to do? He wants to control his environment, his religious environment, and his brother is winning all the time. There is only one thing to do: Put Abel out of the way. Religious people have been disposing of their brothers and sisters ever since - sometimes with Cain's violence, sometimes in more respectable ways - just excommunicating them.

So there is a will-to-power in humanity, sometimes a ruthless will-to-power. Wherever it come from it is born in us. Who ever saw an unselfish baby? Who ever heard one say (or saw it look as if it wanted to say), Dear Mother, I am terribly hungry, but I will not seek your breast till you have had another three hours sleep? Unselfishness is something we have to learn, the selfishness is there to begin with.

So much for original sin. Demythologising does not mean getting rid of myths; it means understanding them. This is of course old stuff among students of the New Testament, and I suspect with us all. Myths are not idle tales; they are ways, often profound ways, of expressing truth, often profound truth, about God and ourselves and our relation with him. For some purposes the myth will serve, for others it will not, and we must demythologise it, expressing the same truth in different style, very often compelled to use ugly abstract nouns in place of its attractive pictures. You will notice that I have been doing it in the last few minutes.

And what of the theory that evolution proceeds by way of natural selection? We know what it means. The giraffe with the longest neck gets the fruit at the top of the tree, and lives; the rest do not get it, and starve. The rhinoceros with the thickest skin charges through the thornbushes and survives; the rest are torn to pieces and die. So long necks and thick skins develop. The man with the best qualifications - or perhaps the best arts at interview - gets the job, and the rest go under. Each one against the rest, each one for himself; and there is original sin demythologised. And it is sound doctrine. Paul knows it, for here precisely is the contrast between Adam and Christ, between the old humanity and the new. It is here in the paragraph of our text, though it has to be dug out and inferred. We know what Adam's act was - the expression of a will-to-power. Christ's corresponding act was an act of obedience; that means a renunciation of personal power. Not what I will, but what thou wilt. On occasion Paul will spell it out in detail. Though he was in the form of God he humbled himself, took the form of a servant, became obedient, even unto death. And all that is neither myth nor dialectic, but history.

I have been all too well aware that so far all this may have sounded more like a theological lecture than a sermon; but we are coming to the sermon, to the preaching of the Gospel, now. And though I disavowed provocation, this may sound provocative enough; for the Gospel is the contradiction of evolution. I do not mean that it rejects evolution as a valid scientific description of the development of creation. Paul can be said to accept it; the biblical picture is of man exercising a will-to-power, putting natural selection into practice. And the will-to-power is God's own intention. The creation narrative itself represents God as saying to the man and woman he has made, "Be fruitful and multiply, and fill the earth and subdue it; and have dominion over the fish of the sea and over the birds of the air and over every living thing that moves upon the earth." The same thought is echoed in the Psalms. This dominion has led to animal and other developments - all good and right when they are rightly used. We owe to man's will-to-power the marvellous advances in our understanding and employment of natural phenomena and processes. But there is a good deal else that we owe to man's will-to-power, from Cain's murder of Abel to Hitler's elimination of the Jews - and much since then. It is this will-to-power, this will-to-survive, this determination to dominate one's environment, that must somehow be dealt with. Dealt with; not eliminated, because if we eliminated it we should case to grow, to learn, to develop - to evolve. We should still tread the earth in deadly fear of the dinosaur, we should squat in our mud huts and think ourselves lucky if we survived to the great age of 21. We would lose Bach and Beethoven, Brahms and Berlioz, Plato and Aristotle, Mommsen and Acton, Barth and Bultmann. But there is stronger reason for holding on not only to any scientific theory that seems to meet the facts but to man's invincible search for mastery over his environment - still striving after knowledge infinite. Stronger reason: it is the command of God. I have quoted it already from Genesis; let me quote it now from the Psalter. "Thou hast made him little less that God, and dost crown him with glory and honour. Thou hast given him dominion over the works of thy hands; thou has put all things under his feet, all sheep and oxen, and also the beasts of the field, the birds of the air and the fish of the sea." I use the Psalm now because it makes explicit what in Genesis is no more than implicit. Recall the beginning of the Psalm: "When I look at the heavens, the work of thy fingers, the moon and the stars which thou has established; what is man that thou art mindful of him, and the son of man that thou dost care for him?" Man, master of his environment, looks small enough when viewed in the context of the universe - even as the universe was understood in antiquity. But the important thing is to see him in the context of God, who established the moon and the stars. "O Lord, our Lord, how majestic is thy name in all the earth! We may fly to the moon and the stars; but God will always outpass our knowledge."

We do not like it. I have already reported - and begun to demythologise - the old story. Man snatches at the snake's temptation: Disobey, eat, and you will be like God. How splendid; he eats, and that is the end of paradise. For as the Prince of Tyre had to learn, "Thou art man, and not God."

But we are not yet at the end of the story. For how does this majestic God behave? We have begun to glimpse this too. The one absolute ruler by right of the total environment of the universe chose to live as a servant; it was in the humiliation of death that he received the name that is above every name, with all creation crying, Lord! So when we meet him we find him in the shame and agony of Calvary, and if we are to live with him we must also die with him. So Paul continues, "Shall we go on in sin, putting down our brother and exalting ourselves, that grace may abound? God forbid; we who died to sin, how shall we go on living in it?" In Christ crucified and risen humanity begins again, and the old adventurous search for knowledge and power is disciplined by love.

PART TWO

Streamed Sessions

INTRODUCTION

The Streamed Sessions provided opportunities for further discussion of the material dealt with in the lectures, as well as the chance to address the topics of science education, movement and Celtic Christianity from an evolutionary perspective.

EVOLUTION THEORY

Professor David Knight

We discussed Lamarck's Theory that all creatures were willing themselves up and on. This led into a discussion about whether or not evolution had an 'upwards' trend. Did species evolve into whatever niche was available, sometimes through 'upwards' evolution, sometimes 'downwards', or was there a general direction? (This point was covered by Rev. Dr. Peacock in the second Gowland lecture later in the day.)

We then had a lively debate about whether evolution could be said to have a purpose. This concluded that we were not all using the terms in the same way! We recognised that since the world is so complex there was uncertainty about outcomes in evolution, was this linked to free will? If we could not predict outcomes, could God?

We talked about two often quoted 'problems' of evolution, the development of the eye and the giraffe's long neck. We found that several different types of eye had evolved over time. Also theoretical studies had concluded that there had been more than sufficient time for the eye to evolve through the process of natural selection.

The group was also comfortable with the idea that during times of food scarcity a giraffe with a longer neck would have improved chances of survival and that this, over the generations, could have resulted in selection for this characteristic.

We considered, when, during the evolution of the species, people first gained a consciousness of God. We talked of the cave paintings and the burial rituals of the Neanderthals. We recognised that death is a mystical event, even in the animal kingdom. We agreed that all knowledge of God comes from God's self disclosure to us and we recalled the progressive revelation seen in the Old Testament. We could not imagine what form an awareness of God might take so many generations before Abraham.

The group drew comfort that over the years many prominent scientists had come to a belief in God through their work and wondered if some current sceptics may find themselves similarly convinced!

HUMAN EVOLUTION

Professor Alan Bilsborough

The group discussed the origins of human populations in various parts of the world, including Australia and Europe; and the importance of contemporary climatic change in understanding the development of human populations was stressed.

The question of the origin of human spirituality arose and whether any evidence can be gained from the fossil record. Professor Bilsborough pointed out that the record could not be expected to provide such evidence directly, but evidence of belief and religion activity could be gained from the manor in which the dead were buried. Cave paintings also provide evidence of thought and perhaps spirituality. In primitive contemporary peoples dream sequences are important and linked to consciousness. In response to a question asking whether the human race has a single origin, Professor Bilsborough suggested the analogy of an evolutionary bush. Growth takes place in a common fashion although the progression of each twig is not predictable. The fossil record can only provide a very limited view of the total picture. Each new find changes our perception of the whole picture. The chances of any one individual being fossilised are remote and the chances of any fossil being discovered even more remote. Nonetheless the fossil record is the best evidence we have but is always subject to review in the light of new findings.

CULTURAL EVOLUTION

Dr. Kate Distin

The group began by posing to Kate Distin some of the questions held over from her plenary session, and this led into a group discussion. Is the Darwinian equivalent of a Cultural Revolution the mutant gene, which causes a discontinuity similar to a paradigm shift - e.g. Mao Tse Tung's revolution, and indeed the coming of Christ to earth? In some ways, yes but the analogy should not be pressed too far.

What about the phrase 'history repeats itself'? Does not this imply that we should be thinking in terms of cultural cycles, rather than steady evolution? In other words, does every meme carry the seeds of its own destruction?

What is the predictive value of gene theory and meme theory? Can we use it to extrapolate into the future? After all, many other scientific theories, especially in physics, are successfully used to predict the future, such as the discovery of new particles. No, what spoils the use of gene and meme theory as a predictor of future events or trends is the salience of the chance factor - the mutant gene.

How is meme theory being applied to practical ends? There are no good examples, which is perhaps somewhat surprising, given how much money and effort is devoted to promoting cultural change in business, industry, local government etc. (e.g. inducing more attention to customer service, quality and safety). It may be that the methods currently used for stimulating such cultural change indirectly utilise some of the concepts of meme theory, but give them different labels.

Can people operate outside their own culture? It is very difficult to do so, because culture is a powerful determinant of human behaviour. However, the ability of individuals to operate outside the culture, e.g. by challenging 'group think', is to some extent assessable by psychometric tests, which are used to identify this characteristic. It may be that the probability of a person 'behaving heretically' is genetically determined.

An example of the difficulty of displaying counter-cultural behaviour is that, because the UK heritage is basically Christian, English children get more interested in other faiths than their own: they think they know all about Christianity because they are locked into the culture.

Is it not arrogant of Christians to claim that they follow the one true way, and thus to imply disparagement of other faiths? Could we not all be humble enough to believe that God speaks to other cultures and faiths differently from our own, and wisely so? An example of the power of humility is the man named Presley, who has walked all the way to Moscow and to the Middle East, to apologise for the wrongs that have been committed by the English in the past, in the name of Christianity. By doing this, he earned great respect from his hosts. It was concluded that Christians would sometimes do better to 'loosen up on their mandate' (to convert the heathen) and open up to those of other faiths.

The group was concerned at the rigidity of church structures and services, which bored children stiff - and not only children but practising Christian adults too. We really need more Christians to speak their minds and challenge the prevailing institutional culture of the church. Perhaps housegroups and other forms of worship than Sunday church (when many families go away at weekend anyway) should be encouraged. It may be counter-cultural, but we need to adapt to social change affecting people's lifestyles.

One member of the group described her experience of going to Mass in Sacré Coeur, Paris. The music had been so uplifting that, despite the Catholicism which was unfamiliar to her, it had transcended all her previous religious experience in church.

Finally, it was concluded that at the present time it is not so much a cultural revolution that surrounds us, but a technological one. We are in the midst of an unprecedentedly wide range of cultural experiences; if only we could see that the purpose of education is to provide access to these rather than imparting mere information, then we would all have a sharper sense of the cultural evolution that is taking place.

MOVEMENT

Mrs. Hilary Barratt

Evolution of Movement

A small select group attended this workshop under the expert guidance of Hilary Barratt! We began at the beginning - our beginning. We curled up and imagined ourselves in the womb, gradually becoming aware of sounds and space and making our first tentative movements. :Later we became aware of more space and found we had to breathe to stay alive. Our mobility increased as we began to roll over, crawl and finally walk on two feet. Our surroundings became increasingly important as we found we could grasp and let go, pile up and knock down. This led to our own childhood memories and a discussion of the games and stories which had had special significance for us.

And finally a few moment of silence as we let the waves of the sea wash over us and we reflected on the wonder of our being.

EVOLUTION OF SCIENCE AND FAITH EDUCATION

Rev. Stuart Roebuck

In the session the issues of working with young people in schools and also with older people were discussed.

In schools the G.C.S.E. syllabus includes bible study, church structure, morals and ethics. There are greater difficulties in teaching cross-curricular issues, such as science and faith which often cause confusion by having answers which are beyond the ability of a particular age group to handle or are open ended. Further difficulties are caused by the technical ways of approaching subjects which permeate our society. Students often find it difficult to apply the materials and approach of one area of study to another. It was noted that although issues such as the big bang theory of cosmology were discussed in religious education very few students at G.C.S.E. and only some at 'A' level felt confident enough to use this material in their essays, children preferring biblical material as the basis of their answers. These areas require the examination of subjectivity and objectivity including creativity, abstract processes which require abilities only just developing in sixth-formers.

Those church members who are not involved in formal education often feel that they have reached the end of their capacity to learn and have feelings of inadequacy in tackling new areas. The church needs to be clear in its aims and to find the most appropriate methods for working with congregations. Three courses were discussed, the Alpha Course (Holy Trinity, Brompton), the Disciple Course and Developing Discipleship (Methodist/United Reformed). The Alpha Course was seen in a positive light although some 20% of the group had reservations. It was seen as a good refresher but did not address the issues of science and faith. Some modification would be needed for this and it was noted that the originators are opposed to any adaptation. The Disciple Course is intensive lasting 34 weeks with a major homework commitment. Developing Discipleship involves 25 sessions.

It was noted that ministerial training on the whole did not address the issue of science and faith although the life experience of many of our congregations means that they have experience of both and that these are the most frequent questions asked by young people when discussing the Christian faith. There are some books available by Paul Davis, John Polkinghorne and Arthur Peacocke.[1]

---

[1] Reference Stanard, R. "The Question Is?", Book and Video, publishers
The Christian Education Movement, price £20.

EVOLUTION OF CELTIC CHRISTIANITY

Leader: Rev. Jamie Mack

History

The Celts moved west from the region around the Black Sea between approximately the 10th and 6th century B.C. to the Brittany area of France; by 4th century A.D. the Christian Church was well established across Europe, and movement was facilitated by the Roman road system.

Evidence exists that wine and pottery originating in the Middle East was used in the Celtic Church around 2nd Century AD.

Following the break-up of the Roman Empire C440-650 A.D., Saxon tribes invaded, much of the Celtic territory, leaving the Celtic tradition in Ireland unaffected. Ninian was the first Celtic Missionary in Mid-West of Scotland (approximating to Solway Firth region).

Patrick was a Briton; he was captured by Irish pirates and was taken to the West of Ireland. There he had a vision which led him to begin his mission to Ireland. In 563AD the Celtic Christian tradition moved to Iona, an island to the west of the larger island of Mull in Scotland. Pure Celtic traditions persisted in remote regions of Cornwall, Wales, North and Scotland.

Theology

Consciousness of nature was one of the strongest elements of Celtic theology. The Celts saw God both as creator, sustainer and redeemer, whereas the Augustinian (Roman) emphasis was on the role of Christ as Redeemer and this contributed to one of the earliest arguments between Celtic Christians and Rome, over Pelagianism. Pelagius, a Celtic monk (360? - 420AD) denied Augustine's doctrine of original sin[1], seeing the newborn baby as innocent[2].

The Celtic approach to evil - God was a protector against external evil. Their position on "internal" evil is not so clear.

Celtic Church Life

Columba stressed both the individual and the corporate or community aspects of the Christian life.

The early Celts chose women leaders in contrast to the Roman church.

There was a natural "wander-lust" among the missionary outlook of the Celts and they were non-confrontational in their mission strategy, looking for positive points of contact. Just as some Greek-speaking Christian Apologists baptised Greek philosophy into Christ, so the Celts "baptised the culture around them into Christ". They followed the spirit of St. John's gospel, Columba claiming "Christ is my Druid" and the standing stones in Scotland being "claimed for Christ".

Celtic Christians brought their prayer into every aspect - the ordinary - things of life. They did not draw sharp distinctions between sacred and secular.

Celtic art is intricate and laden with meaning. The Celtic Warrior Chieftains created in stone and metal a particular style of art with symbolism evident at a deep level. Grooves and curves - (particularly the curves) are evident in the page decoration in Celtic books and works of art.

---

[1] The natural corruption and depravity inherent in the human race because of Adam's first sinful disobedience.

[2] Pelagianism, the body of doctrines held by the followers of Pelagius, who denied original sin, confined grace to forgiveness, and affirmed that human beings' unaided will is capable of spiritual good.

Celtic music rhythm is different from most Methodist church singing rhythm.

The present "Iona Community" is a dispersed community, living all over the world but concentrated particularly in the Glasgow region.

Question

Do the 'Celts' get the Creation aspect a bit out of balance?

Answer

It is a matter of where you start. Most western theology stands heavily on Redemption.

The Catholics wrote the History of the Church in the Mediterranean region, and wrote it from their side.

Response

Pelagius sees a fall "upwards"

Comment

We tend to talk of "personal" salvation and "social" salvation as separate things. Celtic theology sees them as necessarily linked. It takes a holistic view with no distinction between sacred and secular. Celtic Worship looks outward to the world.

The Celtic approach was to build monasteries which were centres of learning in the countryside, contrasting to the city-orientated approach of the Roman church.

Question

Why is there an increased interest in Celtic Christianity?

Answer

We need a sense of spirituality, "Mystery and History". The present church does not offer that kind of spirituality. We need both imagination as well as an emotional and intellectual approach. The History of Celtic Christianity is a mixture of myth and legend, a lot is uncertain.

Printing by
Jiffy Print Limited
9 King Street, Luton, Bedfordshire, LU1 2DW
Great Britain

EVOLUTION OR HOW DID WE GET HERE?
The Eleventh "Christ and the Cosmos" Publication

ISBN 0 9530360 1 4